AT RISK—
NEVER BEYOND REACH

AT RISK—
NEVER BEYOND REACH

Three Principles Every Parent
and Educator Needs to Know

Rabbi Daniel Schonbuch

FOREWORD BY RABBI ABRAHAM J. TWERSKI, MD

leviathan press™

wisdom for the mind, inspiration for the soul™

Leviathan Press
25 Hooks Lane, Suite 202
Baltimore, Maryland 21208
(410) 653-0300 http://www.leviathanpress.com

Cataloging-in-Publication Data
Schonbuch, Daniel.
    At risk–never beyond reach : three principles every parent and educator needs to know / Daniel Schonbuch ; foreword by Abraham J. Twerski. – 1st ed. – Baltimore, Md. : Leviathan Press, 2006.
      p. ; cm.
      ISBN-13: 978-1-881927-34-1
      ISBN-10: 1-881927-34-2
      Includes index.
      1. Jewish teenagers–Conduct of life. 2. Jewish way of life. 3. Child rearing–Religious aspects–Judaism. 4. Parent and teenager–Religious aspects–Judaism. 5. Pastoral counseling (Judaism) 6. Problem youth. I. Title.
BM727 .S36 2006
296.7/4–dc22   0611

PRINTED IN THE UNITED STATES OF AMERICA

Cover design and page layout by Rachel Block.
Copyedit by PeopleSpeak.
Index by Rachel Rice.

Distributed to the trade by Jonathan David Publishers
      (718) 456-8611   **www.jdbooks.com**

Group Sales: Leviathan Press books are available to schools, synagogues, businesses and community organizations at special group rates. Custom-ized books on a per order basis are also available. For information call (410) 653-0300, or email orders@leviathanpress.com.

leviathan press
wisdom for the mind, inspiration for the soul™

To my dear father, Dr. Gerald Schonbuch z"l,
who taught me the meaning of love

Table of Contents

Foreword

I am delighted that Rabbi Daniel Schonbuch has created a new guide for parents that addresses the formidable problem of teens at risk in the Jewish community.

In his concept of Relationship Theory, Rabbi Schonbuch identifies what may be a very significant factor in the problem of kids going astray and a way of preventing that and helping them. It is simply this: *Youngsters need a relationship with someone who they know cares about them (parents, grandparents, teachers, rabbis) and is capable of guiding and assisting them.* This is important even if they appear to reject the guidance.

Economic pressures often necessitate one or both parents putting in so much time at work that they do not have time for a relationship with their children. Tragically, parents may be so busy providing their children with material things and means that they fail to give them the most important gift: *themselves.*

It has been shown that "the single most effective intervention for the widest variety of teen and adolescent problems was also the easiest, speediest, and least expensive: The implementation of family mealtimes."[1] This is because family mealtime fosters relationships.

In this book, Rabbi Schonbuch goes far beyond describing a community problem and its causes. He is able to outline specific techniques readily usable by parents and teachers to prevent religiously unacceptable behavior and to cultivate healthier attitudes in the young. Speaking from his experience as a parent, teacher, counselor, and a keen student of childhood and adolescence, *At Risk—Never Beyond Reach* is a clear and practical book, containing illustrations that are certainly worth "a thousand words."

It gives me a special satisfaction to introduce you to a book that may contribute significantly to the resolution of one of the greatest problems confronting the Jewish family and community.

Rabbi Abraham J. Twerski, MD

Acknowledgments

Special thanks to my wife, Daniella, and my children, Menachem Yisrael, Levi Yitzchak, Esther Faige, Shalom Dovber, and Shmuel and Yaakov Yosef, who have given me so much happiness and joy; thanks also to my parents, Kayla and Zev Brodkin; Dr. Arthur and Jean Schon; Dr. Lew and Erica Schon; Dr. Miriam Gavrin; Rabbi Dr. Tzvi Hersh Weinreb; Moshe Bane; Alan Oirich; Rabbi Kadish Waldman; and Rabbi Shmuel Spero for all their inspiration and support.

I am deeply grateful to Rabbi Abraham J. Twerski, Dr. William Glasser, Chaim Ginot, and the authors of *Motivational Interviewing: Preparing People for Change*, 2nd ed., William Miller and Stephen Rollnick. Their ideas have deepened my understanding of human relationships and allowed me to successfully reach out to countless teens at risk and their families.

Introduction

No teenager is ever beyond reach, especially when parents are willing to learn the key steps that can help them connect to their teenager, improve communication, and respond to their teenager's inner issues. Parents *can* learn how to effectively deal with some of today's most difficult issues, including what to say to a teenager who is struggling with religious identity, engaging in inappropriate relationships, experimenting with alcohol or drugs, or having difficulty in school.

With over twenty years of experience working with teenagers and as a former director of a seminary for teenagers at risk, national educational director of the National Conference for Synagogue Youth (NCSY) of the Orthodox Union, and certified alcohol and substance abuse counselor (CASAC, New York State), I have come to learn a lot about the teenage mind. Now I would like to share some of that knowledge with you.

I firmly believe that despite the challenges, a pathway exists into the hearts and minds of all teenagers at risk based on the principles of Relationship Theory, which states that the most important factors that can influence teenagers' lives are the relationships they develop with their parents, teachers, and other important members in the community. Through focusing on building good relationships and by learning the *Three Cs of Relationship Theory*, connection, control, and communication, parents can begin to wield the considerable influence needed to make a positive difference in the lives of their teenagers.

No one is denying that raising and nurturing teenagers is one of the hardest tasks parents will ever face. It's particularly challenging for religious parents, who are dealing with far-reaching, fast-paced social changes that are making their job much harder. Compounding this are many factors, including work pressures, disintegrating societal values, and a host of conflicting approaches to parenting.

However, the bedrock of successful parenting, as well as of parenting at-risk teenagers, can be summed up in three words: relationship, relationship, relationship. Relationship-based parenting enables parents to become catalysts for dramatic and lasting change by

- Developing lifelong relationships with their teenager
- Motivating without coercion
- Opening new lines of communication
- Creating an environment for long-term emotional growth

The degree of success that parents achieve through reading this book, however, will depend on how much effort they invest in applying the principles, practical suggestions, and procedures. Therefore, in reading this book, parents should not expect to absorb and incorporate every idea at once. Rather, they should take the time to contemplate each new insight and apply the concept to their relationship with their teenagers.

Each chapter is filled with practical parenting advice, including charts and lists that guide parents in responding to at-risk behavior. Also included are excerpts of actual counseling sessions with families and teenagers that show how Relationship Theory helped them deal with many common problems of adolescence, some of which you and your teenager may be facing right now.

1: Searching for the Pill for At-Risk Behavior

© 1999 Randy Glasbergen.
www.glasbergen.com

GLASBERGEN

"Friday night you stayed out until almost 9:00, yesterday you had cola instead of milk and this morning you forgot to floss. Your father and I are afraid you're getting too wild."

L ife is full of stories about teenagers having difficulty making it through adolescence.

However, parenting teens—even teens who are at risk—doesn't have to be such a daunting task when parents are willing to focus more on the relationship and less on getting immediate results. Building the relationship is the key to reaching teens who are at risk.

I understand why most parents feel confused about how to deal with a teenager who veers "off the path." It often comes as a shock when it's your child who is swept into a counterculture that seems to affect more teenagers every day. The "at-risk" phenomenon seems to be everywhere. Although the exact number of teens at risk is unknown, some estimate that the trend touches about one in four religious families. I believe that the numbers are even greater and that the problem likely digs much further into Jewish society than most rabbis, educators, and parents would like to admit.

But what or who is to blame for the at-risk phenomenon? Some suggest that the problem originates in our schools; others maintain that dysfunctional homes are "ground zero" for risky behavior because kids miss out on key emotional ingredients such as love, caring, and parental stability.

Conventional wisdom points to the rapidly deteriorating standards in Western media. Today's television shows, movies, and Internet sites are filled with inappropriate and self-destructive images that are having a negative impact on teenagers and are fueling the at-risk crisis.

However, another possible way of viewing the at-risk phenomenon is that in actuality, it does not exist. Adolescents have always rebelled against the traditions of their parents. The dropout rate among Orthodox Jews is similar to dropout rates in other religious groups that try to maintain higher social and religious standards than the societies they live within.

The theories go on and on, but the problem in our communities and homes continues unabated. David, age sixteen, for example, was a client I saw over a six-month period. Like most of my clients, David came from a traditional Orthodox home and attended a yeshiva in the New York City area. School was always an emotional battleground for David, his teachers, and his parents.

According to David's parents, in fourth grade David started having trouble sitting still in class. He would speak out of turn, disrupt the class, and act in inappropriate ways. He didn't like

Chumash, and his mind would constantly wander. Instead of focusing on school work, he would daydream about video games, movies, and his favorite sports teams. Finding it difficult to concentrate in class was only the beginning of David's problems. In fifth grade, he started getting into fights with his classmates and often received detention for bad behavior. Overall, David was an unhappy and slightly withdrawn child who was about to enter a five-year roller-coaster ride with his parents, principals, and teachers.

Since David was doing poorly in school, his parents decided to send him to a school that specialized in working with teens in crisis. Although his behavior seemed better for a few months, most of David's previous problems remained. He still couldn't sit in class, he didn't like his new classmates, and he began to act out.

David lasted in that school for about a year, but he was still unhappy. Eventually, the situation got so bad that his principal asked David to leave the school.

At the same time, home was a living nightmare for his parents. The boy they had raised to be a well-behaved Shomer Shabbos mensch had turned out to be a loud, unappreciative, and angry teenager. David was in trouble, and his parents were unable to deal with his emotional distress or figure out what to do next.

Their next step was to call their friends, cousins, and rabbis, hoping they would have some insight into the problem. The most common piece of advice given was to send David away or put him in a remedial program. However, David's parents weren't sure what they wanted to do. The tension in the house had become unbearable.

David needed help and his parents needed answers. Most importantly, David's parents needed to know that some glimmer of hope existed, a light at the end of the tunnel that would change their son's life.

Desperate and impatient for a solution, David's parents asked me what the "pill" was for at-risk behavior. I suggested to them that the pill, in most cases, is for parents to start focusing on their relationship with their teenager. I call this novel yet remarkably simple idea "Relationship Theory," which places priority on the power and impact that a good relationship can have upon children, both young and adolescent alike.

According to Relationship Theory, the greater the relationship, the greater the ability parents have to connect to their teenager. Another way of stating this is

$$I = QR$$

where the impact (I) a parent can have is directly proportional to the quality of the relationship (QR) that a parent develops with the teenager.

After all, what better present can parents give than that of themselves? Nothing can beat the pleasure of a true and loving human relationship, a factor that is often overlooked in the increasingly complex and pressurized world in which we live.

The findings of various studies on parent-teen relationships have supported the concept of Relationship Theory. A comprehensive research brief published by *Child Trends*, entitled "Parent-Teen Relationships and Interactions Far More Positive Than Not," showed a direct correlation between the quality of the parent-teen relationship and the impact the relationship has on a teenager's life.

The research showed that positive and warm parent-child relationships were associated with more positive childhood and youth outcomes. Conversely, relationships that were less positive and warm were linked to less desirable childhood and youth outcomes. This pattern persisted across diverse populations, regions, and even countries.

The research brief revealed that

- "Children and teens who have positive relationships with their parents tend to have better academic outcomes."
- "Good relations between parents and adolescents lessen the likelihood that teens will exhibit problem behaviors."
- "High-quality parent-adolescent relationships have been linked repeatedly to mental, social, and emotional well-being in adolescents and youth."
- "Better quality adult child-parent relationships have been associated with lower levels of psychological distress among both adult children and parents."
- "Close relationships with parents during childhood and adolescence have been positively associated with adult children's self-esteem, happiness, and life satisfaction."
- "Positive mental and physical health in adulthood is positively associated with recollections of early parental support."[1]

Building the relationship is often one of the most overlooked aspects of parenting teenagers; yet clearly, as the evidence suggests, the relationship is the key to managing a teenager's at-risk behavior and restoring confidence in the family unit.[2]

Similar conclusions were also reached by two other studies: a Columbia University study in September 2002 found that "isolation from parents make[s] affluent students more likely to become depressed, and to smoke, drink and abuse drugs,"[3] and a National Institute on Drug Abuse study in 1999 showed that "family-focused programs have been found to significantly reduce all the major risk domains and increase protective processes" and that "even those [families] with indicated 'hard-core' problems can benefit from family-strengthening strategies."[4]

To corroborate the findings of these studies, I asked a group of high school juniors and seniors at a well-known Jewish day school what they felt were the most important issues teens face. These were the students' answers according to their own ranking, starting with the most important:

1. Disappointment and anger with parents
2. Dislike of teachers
3. The intense desire to be accepted and fit in with friends
4. The desire to be adults and the fact that they were still under parents' control
5. The internal pressures of trying to develop and act on personal values as opposed to those of parents and friends
6. The powerful forces of media encouraging experimentation with sex and alcohol
7. The enormous physical and psychological changes that occur at this time of life

Surprisingly, issues like physical changes and alcohol use were placed low on the students' list, whereas the issues of poor relationships with their parents and teachers were ranked highest. In general, these teenagers seemed alienated from their parents and felt that their teachers had somehow let them down.

All this information can help parents realize that the cause of teenagers' problems is not necessarily "out there" in the world. Often the source of conflict exists within the boundaries of the relationships teenagers have with their parents, teachers, and friends. Finding ways of deepening their relationships with their teenagers is therefore an important step parents can take to help their teenagers ameliorate their at-risk behavior. The more parents invest in their relationships with their teenagers, the greater chance they will have of making a positive and lasting impression in their teenagers' lives as well.

INVESTING IN YOUR RELATIONSHIP

In many ways, investing in an emotional relationship with a teenager is similar to building a solid financial investment. A wise investment is great preparation for your future, and the formula works for teenagers in exactly the same way, in that the more you put in, the more you can take out. However, any good investment must be carefully planned; time, discipline, and patience are required for you to actually see the fruits of your efforts.

A relationship that has been invested in is one that can endure the many trials and tribulations of adolescence. It's there for you when the going gets tough. So when you need to dig into your investment prematurely, it's waiting for you.

My wife and I try to schedule time alone together with each of our older children at least once a week. Recently, we even started making "dates" with each of our children to go out and have a good time together. Sometimes we go to a restaurant to eat or take a walk. Sometimes we go for a soda at the local convenience store. When life gets hectic and time is limited, I usually spend time reading to or just talking privately with one of my children. Most importantly, during our dates I never talk about homework or behavior problems. We just talk about matters that they think are important.

It really doesn't matter what you do or what you talk about during your private times together. What matters is to give your teenager a feeling that he or she is the most important person in the world. These moments of relationship building give parents the opportunity to develop the kind of personal connection they need to help their teenagers navigate through the turbulent waters of their adolescence.

Although parents often try to force their teenagers to behave the way they expect them to, in the long run, it's not the pressure that parents exert that makes a difference. It's the overall relationship built on a strong sense of friendship that helps teens develop self-esteem and confidence. Self-esteem then becomes a springboard that can help teenagers solve even the most difficult problems.

EXAMINING YOUR PARENTAL VALUES

Imagine a flowing river that is exerting a certain amount of pressure on a levee. Suddenly, without warning a hurricane brings massive amounts of rain placing 50 percent more pressure on the dam. Without an equal amount of stabilizing force being applied to the dam, it won't be able to withstand the new level of pressure against it, and it faces the risk of breaking apart.

Adolescence too can arrive like a hurricane, bringing a "whirlwind" of emotions and putting added stress on a teen-ager's relationships. To meet the challenge, parents need to examine the way they relate to their teenage hurricane. They need to be able to change their style of parenting to endure the new pressures facing their teenagers.

To strengthen the dam, parents must begin by evaluating the core values that define their role as parents. For example, some parents emphasize that their children should do well in school and work hard to achieve professionally. Others want their children to be honest and maintain higher ethical standards of behavior whatever their careers. Some parents believe that their children's most important goal is to be independent and not rely on others for assistance, while others are more concerned that their children maintain their religious identity and avoid the temptations of the outside world.

Although these values are all important in raising children, with a teenager at risk they require moderation. Teens at risk may not be able to achieve intellectually, maintain higher ethical standards, or even live a religious life without a new kind of support system from their parents. The goals that their parents have set for them may be unrealistic. If so, parents need to shift their emphasis toward developing a relationship with their teenager and away from having the teenager live up to their expectations. Instead of professional success or independence as a primary goal, the new center of their parenting must be the relationship.

If you are having trouble with your teenager, you can use figure 1 to try to identify the central tenets that define your parental values. After seeing what lies at the core of your parenting values, look at figure 2, which shows the parenting values prescribed for teens at risk.

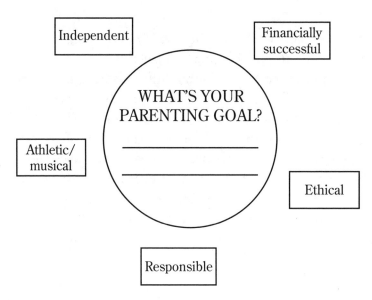

Fig. 1 Your parenting goals

Fig. 2 Parenting goals for at-risk teenagers

The relationship is at the center because the relationship is the single most important (and often most difficult) factor that parents need to work on with their teenager. The relationship must be of primary concern until teenagers are able to make changes necessary to maintain their own stability and fulfillment.

As many parents find out, building a good relationship with a teenager is not a simple task. Often teenagers are reluctant to be close to their parents, and at times they tend to distance themselves as far from them as possible. Teenagers may also be going through various problems that parents need to become aware of if they want to make a difference in their teenagers' lives.

If so, how can parents see beyond the daily power struggles about doing homework, keeping curfew, staying out of trouble, and succeeding in school?

The answer lies in the ability of parents to create a supportive emotional environment that reduces tension, opens new lines of communication, and enhances a teen's self-esteem. Unfortunately, parents often get bogged down in trying to win every battle and lose sight of a much greater picture. But have no fear. In a few years, adolescence will pass and parents will have the opportunity to share a lifelong relationship with their teenager. In the meantime, the challenge is getting through those few years.

Jill Eikenberry, writing in *Parade* magazine, once beautifully encapsulated the dynamics that perhaps all parents raising a teenager experience: "You have a wonderful child. Then, when he's thirteen, gremlins carry him away and leave in his place a stranger who gives you not a moment's peace. You have to hang in there, because two or three years later, the gremlins will return your child, and he will be wonderful again."[5]

Indeed, gremlins have taken the children away, but who or what are the gremlins? A groundbreaking study cited by Dr. Michael J. Bradley in his book *Yes, Your Teen Is Crazy! Loving Your Kid without Losing Your Mind* shed light on the development of the adolescent brain and gave us a clue as to the source and identity of the gremlin.

In 1991, Dr. Jay Giedd of the National Institute of Mental Health took pictures of one hundred teenage brains over nine years at intervals ranging from two weeks to four years. What he found provided insight into the teenage mind. The brain was previously believed to be completely developed by age five or six. Dr. Giedd discovered that throughout the teen years and into the twenties, substantial growth occurs in a brain structure called the corpus callosum, a set of nerves that connects all the parts of the brain that must work together to function efficiently when making decisions. This "wiring" is critical for intelligence, consciousness, and self-awareness.[6]

The study also found that "the prefrontal cortex of the brain goes through a wild growth spurt that coincides with the onset of adolescence whereas the bulk of its maturations occur between the ages of twelve and twenty." The prefrontal cortex is where the most sophisticated human abilities reside, including emotional control, restraint, and rational decision making.

The good news is that parents still have time during adolescence to wire in good qualities like responsibility, learning, achievement, music, and sports. The bad news is that this is a time that may be filled with rage and alienation. Unpredictable thought pathways can outrace judgment capabilities just as they did in early childhood.

The remainder of this chapter describes some of the issues your teenager might be dealing with during this time of rapid change.

Physical and Psychological Changes

Sandy is fifteen years old and doesn't like her body. Her acne drives her crazy. Her body is changing, and she feels overweight. Sandy doesn't know why she gets moody. Somedays she feels happy, and other days she feels down. Sometimes she feels great, while other times she feels overwhelmed and unable to cope with the pressures of school and fitting in with her peers. To the outside world, her concerns may seem petty, but to Sandy they are very real and are constantly on her mind.

Relationships and Premarital Sex

Jack, age seventeen, loves watching videos, especially the ones about male-female relationships. His parents and rabbis keep saying that he shouldn't date girls, but the movies and magazines he sees all support dating and view sexual abstinence as something old-fashioned. Jack wants to get married someday, but his friends say that dating a girl and engaging in physical contact is okay before marriage.

Conflicting Religious Values

Sam, age fourteen, is in conflict with his parents' values. All his life, he and his parents have been active synagogue members, and he always felt he knew the right thing to do. But now some of his friends are pressuring him to come along on Friday nights and party. He wants to be with his friends, but somehow he doesn't feel right about breaking the Sabbath. The difficulty is that he's not sure why. He knows he's not able to be like his parents, but he also doesn't feel good about what his friends do. The real problem is that he doesn't know what he wants!

Learning Disabilities

Fifteen-year-old Steve is in tenth grade and has trouble reading and comprehending books on a seventh-grade level. Steve has a learning disability that makes his life more difficult than the lives of most teenagers his age.

A learning disorder is defined as difficulty in an academic area (reading, mathematics, or written expression). The child's ability to achieve in the specific academic area is below what is expected for the child's age, educational level, and level of intelligence. The difficulty experienced by the child is severe enough to interfere with academic achievement or age-appropriate activities of daily living.

Types of learning disabilities include

- Dyslexia
- Disorder of written expression
- Mathematics disorder

With dyslexia, a child has difficulty learning to read and understand written language. Even children with average or above-average intelligence, plenty of motivation, and ample opportunities to read can have dyslexia. Because children with dyslexia have trouble making the connection between letters and their sounds, they often also have difficulty with spelling, writing, and speaking.

Disorder of written expression is characterized by poor writing skills. And mathematics disorder is a condition characterized by mathematical ability substantially below expectation given a child's age, general intelligence, and education.

An estimated "ten to 30 percent of children have learning disorders. Mathematics disorder is estimated to affect 1 percent of school-aged children. Reading disorders are more common in children of parents who experienced a learning disorder. Boys are more likely to be diagnosed with a reading disorder than girls."[7]

Although the exact reasons for learning disorders are not known, they are believed to involve an abnormality in the nervous system, either in the structure of the brain or in the functioning of brain chemicals. This difference in the nervous system causes the child with a learning disorder to receive, process, or communicate information differently than other children.

Children with learning disorders have an even harder time in schools in which students are required to read and translate at least two languages. For those with a learning disability—especially a reading or language disorder—learning may be a very difficult and unpleasant task. Boys, for example, who can't learn Talmud often feel alienated from religious society and drop out of the religious system altogether.

A large percentage of the teens at risk that I see in my practice have some type of learning disorder, and over the course of their development they have felt progressively alienated from their schools and communities.

Attention Deficit Hyperactivity Disorder

Mark, sixteen years old, has trouble sitting still in class. His mind wanders; he's anxious and is failing many of his subjects. Mark was never tested for attention deficit hyperactivity disorder (ADHD); somehow he slipped through the cracks in the system and never received the help he needed years ago. Mark now faces difficulty finishing high school.

Studies have shown that teenagers with ADHD are at greater risk for school failure, other learning disabilities, and alcohol or other drug abuse. Mark may have more difficulty maintaining friendships and getting along with his family. He may also be more irritable and have a quick temper. Teenagers with ADHD are also at higher risk for developing depression because of the frustrations that come with this disorder.

It is important to note that about "20 to 40 percent of ADHD children may eventually develop conduct disorder (CD), a more serious pattern of antisocial behavior."[8] These children frequently lie or steal, fight with or bully others, and are at serious risk of getting into trouble at school or with the police. They violate the basic rights of other people, are aggressive toward people and/or animals, destroy property, break into people's homes, commit thefts, carry or use weapons, or engage in vandalism.

Depression

Simon, age fifteen, has lost the zest for life he enjoyed as a young child. He is successful in school but personally unhappy. He also suffers from feelings of sadness and despair and has withdrawn from spending time with friends and family. Simon is suffering from depression.

More teens suffer from depression than you might think. It is estimated that one in five children has some sort of mental, behavioral, or emotional problem and that one in ten may have a serious emotional problem. Among adolescents, one in six may suffer from depression. Of all these children and teens struggling with emotional and behavioral problems, a mere 30 percent receive any sort of intervention or treatment. The other 70 percent simply struggle through the pain of mental illness or emotional turmoil, doing their best to make it to adulthood.[9]

I have found that parents do not recognize the symptoms of depression in their adolescent children. Symptoms to look for include

- Constant worry or prolonged irritability
- Lack of energy
- Trouble concentrating
- Wearing dark clothing
- Preoccupation with music that has nihilistic themes
- Chronic aches and pains

Eating Disorders

Rachel has a secret that she is desperate to keep. She's fourteen years old, on the verge of entering high school, and she is dying to be thin, literally. Recently she discovered that maintaining her preadolescent shape might just be possible. Laxative abuse, self-induced vomiting, and excessive exercise may be able to keep her slim forever.

Rachel suffers from bulimia nervosa. She has a serious illness that can lead to malnutrition, electrolyte imbalances, heart attack, and seizures. Some studies indicate that one in nineteen Orthodox teens has an eating disorder, and few receive the care needed to overcome this dangerous and growing phenomenon.

Eating disorders involve serious disturbances in eating behavior, such as extreme and unhealthy reduction of food intake or severe overeating, as well as feelings of distress or extreme concern about body shape or weight. Researchers are investigating how and why initially voluntary behaviors, such as eating smaller or larger amounts of food than usual, at some point move beyond control for some people and develop into an eating disorder. Eating disorders are not due to a failure of will or behavior; they are real, treatable medical illnesses in which certain maladaptive patterns of eating take on a life of their own. The main types of eating disorders are anorexia nervosa and bulimia nervosa. A third type, binge-eating disorder, has been suggested but has not yet been approved as a formal psychiatric diagnosis. Eating disorders frequently develop during adolescence or early adulthood, but some reports indicate their onset can occur during childhood or later in adulthood.

Hating School

Michael is fifteen years old and he's already been to three schools. Last week he was expelled from his yeshiva and is now hanging around at home with nothing to do.

Bearing the pain of the situation and realizing the implications for his future, Michael's parents begin to ask themselves what went wrong. They vaguely remember his early childhood experiences at school. In third grade, he had a hard time with his rabbi. He recalls, "My rabbi was very mean to us. He used to yell at me when I didn't even do anything. He also gave me ridiculous punishments, like writing thirty Mishnayos over and over again—just for coming late to *davening*!"

And then there were the problems in fourth grade and again in sixth grade with the rabbis who Michael's parents thought would understand their son. But he wasn't able to keep up in Talmud, and being frustrated, he just stopped trying. That's when the behavior problems started. Michael started receiving more detentions and notes from the principal, and eventually he got kicked out of school for disrupting the class.

Ask teenagers what they think of school, and these are some of the answers they will give you:

- "The teachers are mean and don't understand me."
- "You don't get to sit next to your friends."
- "I am always singled out and punished, but I didn't do it."
- "The teacher hates me and I hate him."
- "Lunch is too short, classes are too long, and recess is never long enough."
- "There's too much homework."

Now you know more about those gremlins that have captured your teenager. You also know that the gremlins will return your child in a few years. The question is, how are you going to deal with the situation now, while you are waiting?

In the following chapters, we will look at ways of dealing with your teenager's inner issues, how to develop a lifelong relationship, how to motivate without coercion, and how to encourage your teenager to make positive choices in his or her life.

PARENTING TIPS

- Improve the quality of your relationship with your teenager.
- Identify your parenting values and goals, and modify them for a teenager at risk.
- Learn about the common issues your teenager may be facing.
- Realize that many teenage problems subside and therefore you will do best to focus on the long-term development of the relationship.

2: The Three *C*s of Relationship Theory: Connection

© 1996 Randy Glasbergen.
www.glasbergen.com

GLASBERGEN

"At your age, Tommy, a boy's body goes through changes that are not always easy to understand."

Relating to their teenager can be easier than most parents think, especially when they learn about the key areas that can sustain the relationship: connection, control, and communication. Together the Three *C*s of Relationship Theory provide a simple map to help parents evaluate where the relationship is going and show them how to steer their way through the rough roads of the teenage years.

The three *C*s can help parents see the bigger picture and then decide which areas demand attention and which issues are superficial and should not be the focus of their relationship with their teenagers. For example, teenagers may tell their parents one day that they don't want to listen to them and that they are going to do something that the parents disagree with. Or parents may receive an unexpected phone call from the principal to discuss their teen's behavioral problems in the classroom. Should parents become angry, go on the offensive, and try to control their teens' behavior? Or should they try to learn more about their teens' inner issues, spend more quality time with them, and gently counsel them through their dilemmas? A look at the Three Cs should provide an answer.

Most problems can be resolved if parents focus their attention on one or more of the three key areas. According to Relationship Theory, parents need to ask whether the problem can be resolved by connecting more deeply to their teenager, by modifying their level of control, or by improving their communication with their teen.

Figure 3 summarizes the principles of Relationship Theory. In this and the following chapters, parents will learn how to put these principles into action.

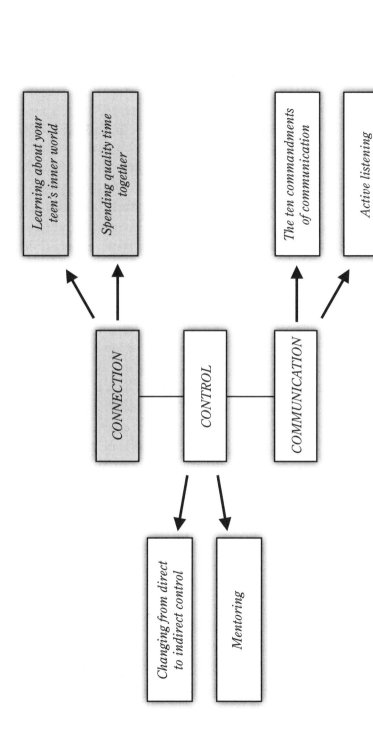

Fig. 3 The Three Cs of Relationship Theory: Connection

CONNECTION

Teenagers have many ways to drive their parents crazy. Take Debbie, for example, a fourteen-year-old girl who attends a prominent Jewish day school. Recently her mother, Nancy, discovered that Debbie had several body piercings concealed under her clothes. Nancy was distraught because her daughter was doing something that she and her husband found repugnant. Nancy found out about the piercings from her neighbor after Debbie slept over at the neighbor's house.

In truth, Debbie's piercings are just one example of various forms of self-abusive behavior that have become trendy. The fashion industry has been able to make body piercing and wearing overly tight clothing or uncomfortable high heels popular. The industry has also created a belief that somehow clothing or accessories will bring a sense of happiness or pleasure to the consumer. Of course, pleasure is a relative term. To Debbie the piercings may have seemed pleasurable since she received attention for being at the edge of fashion. For her parents, however, they were a sign that their daughter was rebelling against their family, and they were causing considerable frustration and embarrassment.

Are the piercings the only problem? Or is something deeper going on in Debbie's life? To help them connect to their teenagers, Relationship Theory asks parents to find out what issues are motivating their teens toward negative or self-destructive behavior.

In Debbie's case, my suspicion was that behind the outer issue of body piercings were deeper emotional issues that related to unresolved conflicts in her family. I believed that her body piercing was a call for help and that her parents needed to find out more about Debbie's inner world.

LEARNING ABOUT YOUR TEEN'S INNER WORLD

Teens like Debbie live in two emotional worlds: an outer world and an inner one. The outer world represents a person's exterior or façade. It is a surface level from which people project their personality to their parents, friends, and society. For instance, in the outer world people can appear friendly and extroverted or sad and uncommunicative. They can also appear defensive or aggressive, but these attitudes don't accurately tell us what's really going on at the core of who they are or what they may be struggling with.

I once saw a client who at first appeared to be very "put together" on the outside. He presented himself as a sharp dresser, considerate, and calm. But after a few minutes of discussing why he had come to see me, it became apparent that he was suffering from depression and anxiety but was carefully hiding this secret from almost everyone around him.

People often try to hide how they feel. But when they do, they may not be aware of how their defensive responses may come across to others—especially their parents. Here is a list of the ways teenagers usually try to hide their feelings that exist below the surface:

- *Negative behavior:* threatening, attacking, sarcastic, rude

  How others perceive this teenager: obnoxious, hostile, aggressive

  Inner feelings: hurt, anxious, embarrassed, fearful

- *Negative behavior:* defensive, shy, withdrawn, uncommunicative.

  How others perceive this teenager: rejecting, suspicious, mistrustful, apprehensive

Inner feelings: angry, resentful, insecure, disappointed
- *Negative behavior:* judging, criticizing, disapproving
  How others perceive this teenager: resentful, bitter, indignant
  Inner feelings: overly self-critical, insecure, angry

Unfortunately, we rely on our outer-world impressions of other people to try to figure out who they are, and that doesn't necessarily give us the full picture of their personalities. It's always helpful for parents to go one step below the surface and explore what's inside their child's inner world. Debbie, for example, presents herself as a rebellious teenager who has a disregard for her parent's religious and cultural sensibilities. She tends to choose clothing that her mother dislikes, and she loves testing boundaries. Through her outer world, Debbie is known for her risky behavior and always seems to be getting into trouble with her teachers. But this is only half the picture. To help a girl like Debbie, we need to go beyond the surface and discover what's really going on inside.

To begin, let's take a look at some of the inner-world issues that exist at the core of teenagers' psyches and may be influencing how the teens behave with their parents. Although many theories describe this hidden world, we'll focus on several areas that can be addressed by parents.

The five dimensions are self-esteem, individuality, love and friendship, control, and meaning. As we explore each of these categories, parents should try to evaluate whether or not they are responsive to these specific emotional needs. A short relationship test question appears at the end of each section to help parents understand the strengths and weaknesses in their relationship with their teenager.

Self-Esteem

We often use the expressions "good self-esteem" or "poor self-esteem" to describe people's evaluation of their own worth. When people have good self-esteem, they tend to view life from a positive perspective, seeing their potential value. Poor or low self-esteem causes people to feel that everything they do in life is a losing battle and that they always get the short end of the stick.

Low self-esteem can be very painful and difficult to overcome. Self-esteem is something we come into the world with; it follows us through life like a shadow. If we lose it, we are lost. If we have it, we can face all of life's trials and tribulations and maintain our sense of satisfaction and emotional well-being.

Self-esteem is also profoundly affected by what happens to us along life's path. Many circumstances may contribute to low self-esteem in teenagers, including

- Divorce
- Learning disabilities
- Lack of friendships
- Illness
- Physical or emotional abuse
- A sick parent
- A death in the family

Many of these issues make a person feel that life will always be fraught with pain and failure. Low self-esteem makes people feel that their proverbial cup is always half empty.

For parents trying to connect to teenagers with low self-esteem, the best strategy is not to focus on the teens' negative patterns of behavior but rather to find ways to nourish their inner sense of self. Parents can take many steps to help build their teens' self-esteem. Here are just a few:

- Highlight positive aspects of their physical, mental, and emotional development, such as the way they look, the way they express their thoughts and feelings, the skills they have, and those they are developing.
- Focus on their accomplishments. Congratulate them for their achievements, however big or small. Remind them daily of the things they do well and of the courage they have shown.
- Help them to be realistic and accept the facts that they aren't perfect at everything and they don't have to be.
- Teach them to laugh at past disappointments when you can. Use setbacks as opportunities for insight and growth.
- Help them develop a support system of people they trust who will listen when they need to talk.

RELATIONSHIP TEST

Do you take time to develop your teen's self-esteem?

1	2	3	4	5
Never		Rarely		Constantly

Individuality

A person's individuality consists of the qualities and characteristics that distinguish that person as a unique human being. Without a sense of uniqueness, it is difficult for a person to establish his or her own identity in the world and to understand the special role that he or she will play.

Individuality is a very powerful part of being a teenager, and the need for it grows as children get older. Young children's identities are often enveloped in the family's identity, and they have little opportunity to express their own sense of self. But as they become teenagers, they have a greater need to establish their unique identity among their family and peers.

For teens at risk, parents need to take the time to acknowledge their teenagers' unique positive qualities. Unique qualities distinguish every human being. The fact that a teen may be depressed or difficult to relate to does not mean that the teen has no positive personality traits that need to be highlighted. For example, a fifteen-year-old girl who is doing poorly in school excels as an artist and musician. Or a fourteen-year-old boy with ADHD is a talented carpenter and has many practical and social skills that will help him to succeed in the business world.

Unfortunately, we tend to demand the same level of success academically from all children, even though school achievement may not be an appropriate measuring stick with which to evaluate their success in life. Try to look at all teenagers as diamonds that need to be polished. When you help identify people's unique qualities, you are helping them to remove their rough exterior and allowing their G-d-given brightness to shine.

At the same time, a teen's individuality must be moderated in relation to many other factors, including the need to be part of the family, the school, and society. The challenge of individuality is for parents to nurture their teens' sense of uniqueness and at the same time help them to integrate their identity into the greater whole.

RELATIONSHIP TEST

How often do you help your teen become aware of his or her individuality?

1	2	3	4	5
Never		Rarely		Constantly

Love and Friendship

Love is one of the most important ingredients of life that can contribute to a person's emotional well-being. It is experienced when a person senses feelings of affection and fondness from others, especially from family and friends.

Children begin life seeking love from their parents and their environment. When babies are fed when hungry, held when scared, and covered when cold, they sense feelings of love and security from their parents. If the desire for love is fulfilled, children can grow up with the confidence needed to live a life of optimism and emotional security. If the need for love is frustrated, then children can be left with feelings of loneliness and despair.

Although we usually think about love as a necessity for young children, teens also need the same special feelings of love and affection from their parents as they get older. The way love is expressed by parents, however, may need to be changed according to the various stages in teens' lives. Love for teenagers does not mean buying them a lollypop or allowing them to stay up a little longer. Love for most teenagers is best expressed when parents are able to understand their needs and are willing to listen to their inner issues. For a teenager, "to understand me" means "to love me."

Although teens aren't always easy to deal with and your relationship with your teenager may be strained, it's crucial to continue to express feelings of love and kindness and give your child a sense that you care about him or her. More than anything else, teenagers at risk need friendly and loving parents who are able to spend enjoyable time with them without criticizing them or making them feel that they are being unjustly controlled.

RELATIONSHIP TEST

How often do you nurture your teen's need for love and friendship?

1	2	3	4	5
Never		Rarely		Constantly

Control

As children move from infancy into middle and later childhood, they have a growing need for control over their environment. To meet this need, teenagers must be given reasonable power to make choices about what they eat, whom they play with, and what extracurricular activities they participate in. They need to be given the opportunity to make choices that they view as important in different areas in their lives. Parents can find many ways to safely empower teens without allowing them to make dangerous choices. Teens can make safe choices when buying clothing, planning family trips, or selecting their birthday presents. Most of the time, the significance of the choices does not matter; even small decisions can make a difference and allow teens to feel that they can fulfill their desire for control in a healthy way. Whether to eat chocolate or vanilla ice cream, what time to have a get-together, or which days are best for a family outing are equally important. Although some choices seem inconsequential, what matters is the overall feeling teenagers will have when given the power to choose.

I once counseled a family whose oldest child had trouble sitting for a long period of time at the Shabbos table. As the firstborn, he seemed to have a strong desire for control and felt too old to be sitting with his younger brothers and sisters. I suggested to his father that he make his son a partner in running the Shabbos meal and turn over some responsibility, such as giving out treats to the other children for good behavior. Almost immediately, this teenager felt empowered at the table and was more willing to participate and enjoy the family experience. He was provided a way to fulfill his need for control in a healthy manner, which reduced the power struggle that had been going on for some time at the table.

Control may also be given in return for a teen accepting increased responsibility. Here are some suggestions for safe levels of control parents can allow their teenager:

- For teenagers who want to use the car: Make a list of necessary maintenance activities, like buying gas, changing the oil, and checking the pressure in the tires. Explain that when you see that they are responsible for taking care of the car, you will discuss ways of letting them use it more often.

- For teenagers who want to buy their own things: Open a bank account with them and set target dates for saving money to buy the items they want. You can also deposit an allowance into the account on a weekly basis according to their behavior in the home.

- For teenagers who want to have more fun outside the house: Make a list of chores around the house that they are responsible for. Reward their performance monetarily or by taking them to do fun things.

- For teenagers who want to buy a lot of clothing: Create a monthly clothing allowance, a budget, and a list of prices of the clothing they want to buy.

- For teenagers who don't like school and want to work: Arrange for an after-school internship in a local business or profession.

- For teenagers who don't like eating with the family: Buy an easy cookbook and have them make a weekly menu of the foods they prefer. They can also help cook the meals they have chosen.

When parents empower teenagers with a healthy modicum of control, they are giving them the strength to step into the adult world and take responsibility for their own actions.

RELATIONSHIP TEST

How often do you give your teenager the opportunity to make his or her own choices?

1	2	3	4	5
Never		Rarely		Constantly

Meaning

The fifth component of the inner world is what the eminent psychiatrist and Holocaust survivor Victor Frankl called the "Will to Meaning."[1] This desire for meaning implies wanting to know the whys of life and not just the hows.

Most teenagers have a tremendous desire to know why events are happening to them. In fact, when teens are empowered with meaning and understand the whys of life, they are more able to negotiate the hows and the many challenges that life presents.

Unfortunately, our educational system often denies a teenager's need for meaning. Our schools tend to tell our children *what* they have to do but not *why* they have to do it. When they are given an answer like "because I said so," they interpret it to mean that the teacher is not interested in what they are feeling or what they have to say.

With this in mind, parents need to spend a considerable amount of time trying to explain to their teens the whys of life. For example, when children feel neglected by their school, parents can help by discussing with them how a school runs, the financial and organizational pressures facing the school, and why teachers can't always give students the attention they deserve.

Teenagers also benefit from knowing the meaning behind their parents' behavior. If you want your teenager to go to bed early, for example, the reason you might offer is that the teenager has been working hard all day and needs to go to sleep early. And that's sufficient. At least your teenager knows why you expect him or her to go to sleep and does not think that you simply don't want him or her around.

I remember coming home from a very hard day of work to a very lively household of children. I told them that I needed a break and would be glad to play with them later in the evening. In the past—before I learned about my children's inner desire for meaning—I wouldn't have spent much time explaining to them how I was feeling. After learning more about their inner world, I was able to sit down with my two older boys and say, "I just want you to know that I love you very much and I had a really pressured day at work. I have a big headache and need some time to read a book and relax. Giving me a little time now will allow me to give you more quality time later. Please play by yourselves for another half hour. Then I will come out and help you with your homework and play." When I explained to them why they couldn't have my immediate attention, they were much less hurt by my not spending time with them.

Parents shouldn't worry that they have to provide the perfect answer for every question or know the meaning behind everything that happens in life. Nor do their answers have to be absolute proof in the philosophical sense. If parents don't feel that they have the right answers, they can always tell their teenagers that they would like to speak to an expert in that field or do some more reading about the topic. The key element is to make teenagers aware that you are interested in their world and willing to discuss ideas that are close to their hearts.

RELATIONSHIP TEST

How often do you explain to your teenager the whys of life?

1	2	3	4	5
Never		Rarely		Constantly

The Relationship Test

Now go back and add up your numbers for all five of the relationship tests. The test is a measuring stick that can help you evaluate how responsive you are to your teen's needs. If you scored below ten, then clearly the bonds of your relationship are very weak and you need to spend time nurturing your connection. If you scored above ten, then you have a greater chance of breaking through into your teen's emotional world. If you scored twenty or above, then you are doing a great job and you should continue to strengthen the quality of your relationship.

By focusing on their teens' inner worlds, parents can create a deeper connection and facilitate a greater sense of

closeness. The benefits of this new relationship include
- Mutual respect and trust
- Empathy—sympathetic understanding—for one another
- Emphasis on assets rather than faults
- Sharing of thoughts and feelings rather than hiding them and bearing resentment

Spending Quality Time Together

As part of the process of connecting to your teenager, an important step is spending quality time together. I know that for many families, spending time with an individual child or teenager seems like a daunting task. However, making the effort to do so can go a long way in building your relationship.

One of the questions that parents have is about what will happen if they spend time alone with a teenager with whom they fight. The answer is often surprising. Most teenagers enjoy the special occasion of spending time with their parents alone, especially outside of the home. I counsel many families who have daily screaming matches with their teenagers, but when they take them out of the house, the emotional environment can change very quickly.

During this time with their child, parents should try to imagine that they are going out on a date for the first time. Everyone knows that the first time people meet someone else, they are careful with their emotions. They know that they have to be calm and pay special attention to not delve into the other person's private matters. A kind of healthy distance exists that protects people when they first meet and helps them to maintain a sense of awe and respect.

When you are alone with your teenager, it's important not to rehash the same issues you have been fighting about in the home. Talking about general ideas concerning current events, music, or sports or about your child's feelings regarding life and relationships is more productive. The main idea is to have a good time together. Work on developing conversation in the way that you would with a friend.

Many parents think that the only way to get their teenager to spend time with them is by shopping or eating out. But that is not entirely true. I suggest parents connect with their teenagers by finding hobbies and activities of common interest. For example, my wife and I found a pottery studio nearby where parents and children can paint kitchen items like coffee mugs and tea pots that are then professionally produced in a kiln. Painting pottery is a simple and fun way of spending time together. You can also share what you painted with the rest of your family to symbolize the productive nature of spending quality time with your children.

Seventy-Three Activities You Can Do with Your Teenager

Let's take a look at many positive ways of spending time together:
- Make dinner.
- Learn a hobby.
- Make popcorn and talk.
- Adopt an elderly neighbor and carry out some chores for him or her, or visit from time to time.
- Organize a recycling project.
- In the winter, arrange through the school a collection of blankets for the homeless.
- Participate in a fun run/walk.
- Do a jigsaw puzzle.
- Build a model car or airplane.

- Take a walk around the neighborhood.
- Visit a *matzah* factory.
- Go on a nature walk.
- Clean out the garage, and then celebrate a job well done!
- Go to a Jewish concert.
- Go to the library.
- Visit a major harbor.
- Learn Torah.
- Go to the Jewish Community Center.
- Play computer games.
- Visit your workplace.
- Talk about planning a career.
- Get together with friends from work.
- Visit a home for the elderly.
- Visit Hatzolah, the Jewish emergency medical services.
- Go RollerBlading.
- Go to a museum.
- Take a personality test (on the computer).
- Take photos of favorite people or places.
- Conduct a pretend job interview.
- Listen to each other's favorite music together.
- Talk about how to get a job, and then look for a part-time job.
- Check out the work experience program at school.
- Balance a checkbook.
- Visit your old school.
- Talk about balancing work and play.
- Play a sport together (e.g., basketball, volleyball, golf, baseball, football).
- Open a bank account.
- Talk about budgeting.

- Visit a sick child or hospital patient.
- Go bargain hunting.
- Plan a week's worth of meals.
- Do a week's grocery shopping.
- Go holiday shopping.
- Write thank-you notes.
- Go to *shul*.
- Talk about relationships.
- Build, create, or design something.
- Paint a house or picture.
- Fix an appliance.
- Talk about personal values.
- Draw your family tree.
- Talk about the future.
- Plant and maintain a vegetable garden.
- Visit the police station or fire department.
- Write a song.
- Do good deeds for three strangers.
- Have a picnic (at a nearby lake, zoo, park, mountain).
- Take a ferry ride.
- Take a train ride.
- Fly a kite.
- Go hiking or kayaking or camping or sailing.
- Go fishing.
- Play with a Frisbee or participate in some other fun outdoor game.
- Play board games or cards.
- Mow your lawn.
- Create a journal, including photos, of your times together.
- Start a collection (e.g., stamps, coins, or whatever is the craze at the time).

- Go ice skating.
- Arrange a visit for your teenager to meet significant personalities in your neighborhood.
- Attend a cultural festival.
- Visit city hall or a local council meeting.
- Arrange a garage sale.
- Offer to help serve meals to the homeless or to help at a shelter for people in need.

CONNECTING IN PRACTICE

The following conversations illustrate how a little time and knowledge can go a long way toward establishing a connection with your teenager.

Debbie's Body Piercing

Referring back to our earlier case of Debbie's body piercing (page 26), let's see how I used knowledge of Debbie's inner world and the power of spending quality time together to help her parents connect to her, as the following dialogue demonstrates.

Daniel Schonbuch (DS): I'm interested in finding out more about your relationship. Was there a time when it was better?

Mother: Actually, Debbie and I never had a great relationship, although it used to be better when she was younger.

DS: When did it change?

Mother: Well, I think it started to get bad around the time she turned eleven. She was always a quiet girl and didn't talk much about her feelings. When her body started changing and she started putting on weight, she started feeling terrible about herself.

DS: Would you say that Debbie has low self-esteem?

Mother: Absolutely. It's something she has been struggling with for years.

DS: Is she the kind of teenager who feels that nothing goes right in her life?

Mother: I think so. She is always complaining about school, teachers, her sisters, and her friends.

DS: Tell me a bit about her friends.

Mother: I don't like her friends very much. They are always getting into trouble with boys and things. She spends all night talking on the phone with them. Last night she was up until two o'clock talking, and I couldn't wake her up this morning.

DS: Do you often fight about things like waking up or going to bed?

Mother: All the time. It's gotten so bad that I try not to fight anymore with her. But what can I do? Let her fall apart?

DS: What about the way she dresses?

Mother: I think it's terrible. Debbie always looks shlumpy, like she doesn't care that much about how she looks.

DS: She doesn't care about her looks?

Mother: She doesn't know how to present herself to others. It seems that she always picks something a little out of fashion to wear. It's like she's saying, "Don't bother me with fashion statements."

DS: Do you also fight about her clothing?

Mother: Of course. We've been fighting for years about her clothes. The more I get involved in her clothing, the more we just end up fighting with each other.

DS: Do you ever take her out to go shopping?

Mother: I try, but she is impossible to buy clothing with. Last week I took her for a pair of shoes for our cousin's bar mitzvah, and she kept saying, "I can't stand these shoes. You don't know what I want!"

From this conversation, it seemed that Debbie was dealing with two main issues: self-esteem and control. I wanted to see if we could find a creative way to address her inner need for control and work to build up her self-esteem. I also wanted to try to reduce the tension in Debbie's and her mother's interactions and start moving their relationship in a positive direction.

DS: Let me ask you a question. Does Debbie have a clothing allowance? Do you spend money on her clothes?

Mother: She doesn't have an allowance; she just gets things when she needs them. We don't have enough money to support an allowance fund. It's hard enough just making ends meet.

DS: Okay, let me make a suggestion. Why don't you try to make a budget? I know things are hard for you, but I'm sure you already spend money on her clothing. Work out with your husband how much you could be sure of being able to give her every month. Tell her that you and her father think it is a good idea. But remember, don't say anything about the body piercing. The goal is to empower her and give her a good feeling about herself. You can't really control her anymore, but you can make her feel that you care about her.

Mother: It's not a bad idea.

DS: I hope that she will feel you are supporting her.

Mother: We have been fighting for so long. I don't know what it will do.

DS: It's not what it will do, it's about the feeling that you will give her. The unconscious message is "I just want you to feel good about yourself. Here's some money so you can buy something pretty that you enjoy." You also need to address her need for control. I want to see if this approach can help.

The next time Debbie's mother returned, she reported to me that Debbie liked the idea of having a clothing allowance. I asked her mother to try this out for a few months and be very careful not to criticize Debbie about her clothing. During that time, I wanted to talk to Debbie about her feelings of low self-esteem and asked her if she would consider coming in to talk with me.

Debbie agreed to come, and over the next few months we talked about the difficulties she was having relating to her parents and how much she hated school. What emerged was that Debbie had never really spoken with anybody about her inner-world issues. She had a lot of built-up anger that was now directed at her mother. As I had suspected, Debbie was acting out her frustrations by trying alternative behaviors, like body piercing.

In truth, her body piercing was a sign that she was in trouble, and my goal was to allow Debbie to work out her issues in a positive way and to help Debbie's parents establish a better relationship with her.

To accomplish this, I made the following suggestions:

1. Schedule a weekly time to spend with Debbie outside of the home, and choose some of the seventy-three suggestions for fun activities listed on pages 40–43.
2. Address Debbie's need for control by rewarding her for fulfilling responsibilities in the home.
3. Find a tutor to help Debbie do better in school.
4. Explore and nurture Debbie's potential talents.

Over the next year, I continued to talk with Debbie and her mother about strengthening their relationship. I tried to convey to both Debbie and her mother that if they could work to become slightly warmer to one another, they might actually enjoy their relationship and begin to support each other through this difficult emotional period in their lives.

After working hard to free up spare time, Debbie's parents began to schedule weekly outings alone with Debbie. They also discovered that Debbie was interested in pursuing her talents in art and design and hired a tutor to give her private lessons in computer graphics and web design. Gradually, both sides seemed interested in making the relationship better, which was a sign that the situation could improve.

Recently Debbie's mother called to tell me that Debbie had spoken to her about her body piercing. Surprisingly, Debbie had been willing to speak openly about her body issues and said she was just experimenting and had taken out the pierced jewelry several weeks before.

Although the body piercing was the original issue of contention, it proved to be a catalyst for Debbie and her family to resolve deeper and more fundamental inner emotional issues. Debbie's parents felt more confident in their ability to deal with a situation that they had believed was out of control. Improving the relationship was the key to helping Debbie with a difficult and painful time in her life.

Toby's Secret Dating

Recently a woman named Ruth came to my office to talk about her fourteen-year-old daughter. Ruth comes from a mainstream Orthodox family and has five children. Her middle child, Toby, was in her sophomore year at a yeshiva high school for girls in the New York City area.

Ruth explained to me that her daughter had been secretly dating a boy for over a year. Ruth had recently found out about this from the parents of one of Toby's friends. Ruth had confronted Toby about her boyfriend, but Toby had adamantly refused to admit that she was secretly seeing anyone. Ruth was extremely distraught to realize that her daughter would do something against her wishes and asked if I could help.

Since Toby was dating a boy against her parents' will, I was especially interested in understanding Toby's relationship with her parents. Perhaps Toby's inner desire for love and friendship was somehow unfulfilled and she was starting to look for love in the wrong places.

The following is one of my conversations I had with Toby's mother.

> *DS:* Could you tell me a little bit more about her relationships with you and your husband?
>
> *Ruth:* Well, Toby and I don't get along very well. We do have some pleasant moments together—especially when she wants me to give her something like money—but most of the time we are always fighting. It's impossible to get along with her. Sometimes she makes me so angry I get a headache.
>
> *DS:* It sounds rough. What about your husband? Are things better or worse with him?
>
> *Ruth:* Her relationship with him is even worse. They barely talk to one another, and when they do they start yelling at each other.
>
> DS: What are they fighting about?

Ruth: Almost everything. He fights with her about the way she dresses. He doesn't like her friends. And he is very angry that Toby doesn't join the family at Shabbos meals.

DS: Do you and your husband ever spend any time with her without fighting?

Ruth: Once in a while when we go out for dinner at restaurants, she seems to calm down with us.

DS: I guess she feels that you are treating her to something special.

Ruth: That is true. When we go shopping together alone, things also seem to calm down slightly, as long as we are doing something out of the house. But the minute we are home it seems to get worse. When my husband comes home, it can be unbearable.

DS: Unbearable? Tell me more about your husband. What is he like with her? When does he come home at night?

Ruth: My husband is another story. He is very stressed out and almost never home. He runs a business— a car dealership.

DS: It sounds like he is very busy.

Ruth: Yes, it's terrible. Even on Shabbos he is so stressed out and withdrawn. When he comes home after *shul*, he makes Kiddush, eats, and goes to sleep. The kids want to talk to him, but they see that he's too irritable to deal with. I don't want to push him too much. I'm worried he'll explode.

DS: How about Toby? Does she get to spend any time talking to your husband?

Ruth: Not really. Even if he had some free time, he doesn't know how to communicate with her without fighting.

As I had suspected, a problem about an outer-world issue—a secret boyfriend—pointed to a hidden inner issue, the lack of love and friendship. I wanted to try to move our discussion in a positive direction by focusing on Toby's relationships in her family. We would eventually discuss the boyfriend, but we needed to wait until we could build a sense of trust in the family.

DS: Ruth, from what you have described to me, it seems that Toby is lacking something in her relationships. Although she seems to want to do her own thing, I think that what she is really crying out for is a deeper relationship with you and your husband. I know you love her very much and would do anything to help. I'm sure your husband feels the same way. What I want to try to do is to reduce some of the tension in the house and see if we can improve the quality of the relationship. Both of you play an important role in her life. You can give her a sense of warmth and security. It seems that Toby needs her father to be more involved in her life. She needs to feel that she is loved by him and that she can talk to him without feeling judged or criticized.

Ruth: So what can I do?

DS: There's a way to help Toby. It's called Relationship Theory, which states that the most important way for parents to show their love for their teenagers is by developing their relationships with them. Often the emergence of emotional problems like Toby's is a sign that a child is missing a critical relationship—most likely with a parent. If you can build that relationship, then a lot of pain and stress can be alleviated.

During the next few sessions, I slowly tried to bring the father into the picture. I also recommended that Ruth and her husband plan a one-day outing with their daughter. The goal was to get away and just have a lot of fun. I thought a boat ride or trip to the country would be the easiest way for the family to share precious moments together without fighting and without tension. I explained to Ruth that the most important goal during the trip was to avoid critical language. No matter what Toby said, Ruth and her husband must respond only in a loving way. If they wanted her back, Toby's parents needed to be able to listen to her and make her feel that she was loved unconditionally.

After the trip, her parents reported to me that they believed the time together with her had slightly improved their relationship. Toby had enjoyed the personal attention from her parents. Just spending time alone with her was a sign to Toby that her parents really cared about her. Not criticizing or fighting with her sent Toby the signal that her parents cared more about her than about what she did.

During that time, I also began to see Toby on a weekly basis, and we discussed her emotional history together. Toby had been having trouble in school from sixth grade onward. According to Toby, when she was about eleven years old she started experiencing feelings of rage and began disliking her teachers and her friends. At about the age of thirteen, she started becoming interested in boys and began looking for boys who might be interested in her. Toby also started staying out late at night with boys and girls who were having similar problems with their parents.

From her description, it sounded as if Toby's desire to spend time with boys was rooted in a deeper desire for closer relationships. Over the next few sessions, I worked with Toby and her parents to see if Ruth and her husband would consider trying a different style of parenting and if Toby would be willing to give them a chance. This was not going to be easy. Both Toby and her family had developed rigid patterns of communication, and life at home was tense.

I worked to help Toby's parents become more sensitive to her inner-world issues, such as the need for control. I suggested the following actions:

1. Allow Toby to gain some form of control in her life by giving her a clothing allowance.
2. Empower Toby by giving her the opportunity to work helping younger children in various *chessed* projects in her community.
3. Build Toby's self-esteem and sense of individuality by making a list of Toby's potential talents in music, art, or athletics and nurturing them.
4. Plan several outings alone with Toby, and allow her to choose the types of fun activities that she would like to do.

The goal was to look at Toby's good traits and to make sure that they were given a chance to grow. By doing so, her parents would be signaling to her that they were not merely interested in their own agenda but focused on treating Toby as a unique individual.

In the process, they discovered that Toby desired to work with young children. They then arranged for her to work in an after-school day-care program in which Toby could utilize her skills and learn how to contribute toward the greater good of the community.

By introducing Relationship Theory, we were able to open new lines of communication. Eventually, Toby started talking to her parents about her boyfriend. She first needed to see that other loving relationships were possible and that her parents were willing to extend themselves toward her in a loving way. Toby's parents were also pleased that their relationship had improved. They were hopeful that their daughter would continue to feel more comfortable about allowing them to help her through these painful emotional issues. Eventually Toby decided not to see her boyfriend anymore.

Addressing the inner issues of control, self-esteem, and individuality was the key to helping Toby resolve her dilemma about premature dating and help her get through one of the most difficult periods in her life.

PARENTING TIPS

- Examine your teenager's inner issues.
- Look for hidden feelings behind your teenager's words.
- Highlight positive aspects of your teenager's personality.
- Express your love through words and actions.
- Give your teenager control combined with responsibility.
- Address your teenager's need for meaning.

3: The Three *C*s of Relationship Theory: Control

Copyright 2000 by Randy Glasbergen.

—GLASBERGEN

"I CAN'T GO TO THE MOVIES WITH YOU, ELENORE. I'M STILL GROUNDED FOR SOMETHING I DID IN 1937!"

In our rapidly changing world, the idea of control has begun to change more quickly than anyone can imagine. A metamorphosis of unparalleled proportion is taking place, and many parents feel that they are unequipped to deal with the challenges that it will demand.

Not too long ago, parents could maintain a fair amount of control by limiting their children's access to the outside world. For example, when I was young, a teenager had to watch television or go to a movie theater to see the latest show. However, with the advent of home videos, teens could choose their own movies and watch them when their parents were out or went to sleep. Then the Internet came along. For the first time, children of all ages could choose anything they wanted to see or hear. Some parents chose to fight back by purchasing Internet blockers that filtered out inappropriate content. But what happened when their child was visiting someone else's home and wasn't being supervised?

The story doesn't end there. Suppose parents can control what their children watch at home and with whom and where they play until they're adults. Until recently, that might have worked. But now, with the latest wireless technology that enables rapid transfer of sound, pictures, and movies, the power of control has been taken away from parents and given to teenagers who can watch whatever they want, wherever they want. As communications become faster and more portable, parents can find themselves losing more and more control every day.

Parents may still want control, but their strategy may have to change. In order to maintain equilibrium (and their sanity), parents need to shift into a new mode—a mode beyond the traditional understanding of control—and enter the world of Relationship Theory.

As illustrated in figure 4, the second *C* of Relationship Theory reminds us that in order to have more emotional impact, parents need to moderate the way they control their teenagers. This necessitates a shift from using direct control to influencing behavior through indirect control.

Direct control, or what Dr. William Glasser in *Unhappy Teenagers: A Way For Parents And Teachers To Reach Them,* calls "external control,"[1] is an attempt by parents to impose their will on their teenagers. For example, if a child refuses to do homework, a parent who uses direct control will say, "If you don't do your homework, you will not go out with friends, receive an allowance, or be allowed any more treats

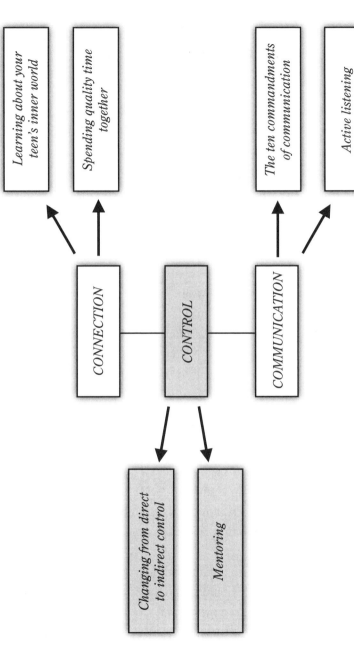

Fig. 4 The Three Cs of Relationship Theory: Control

on Shabbos." Direct control is a powerful mechanism used by parents to get what they want regardless of the emotional effects of their actions.

Indirect control, or influence, however, can be achieved by parents looking into *why* their teenager isn't doing homework and trying to address the cause and not merely the symptom. It's all about addressing inner needs and being less focused on a teenager's accomplishments.

As Rabbi Abraham J. Twerski, M.D, explains in his book *Successful Relationships at Home at Work and with Friends: Bringing Control Issues Under Control*, "Everyone may have the need to wield control, and there are many relationships which may indeed require control. Exceeding an acceptable amount of control invites trouble."[2]

Parents who aim to wield too much direct control are often viewed by their teenagers in a negative light. Most teenagers would say that a controlling parent is manipulative, destructive, and unable to relate to them in a meaningful way.

People, including teenagers, suffering from a controlling relationship are likely to hold one or more of the following illusions:

- They are stuck with another person's definition of them.
- They do not have the right to their own opinions.
- They can earn love and acceptance by abdicating control to another person.
- They are "successful" if they fulfill another person's vision, even when it does not in any way support their own.
- They must obtain permission to act in matters that are, in fact, their own business.

Controllers struggle to shape the lives of others and often destroy the relationships that they want most to preserve. They usually don't realize the senselessness of their own behavior.

Most parents don't believe that they are controlling. This is because they are used to wielding a considerable amount of control over what their children do, so it seems normal. Control to that degree *was* appropriate from birth to around the age of nine or ten, when children needed to be given healthy boundaries and to be pointed in the right direction. But troubled teens need something different. They feel that they have grown beyond their parents' control and that their controlling parents are living in the past.

When direct control is released, parents may experience a different kind of relationship—one that seemed to have been lost a long time ago. Some parents even report that giving up direct control was like giving birth to their child for a second time. When parents give up control, they are actually giving life to a more mature and meaningful relationship.

CHANGING FROM DIRECT TO INDIRECT CONTROL

The change from direct to indirect control can also influence the way parents discipline their teenagers. So many opinions exist on the issue of discipline that many parents often don't know which way to turn. For example, some schools of thought suggest a "tough love" approach while others advise parents to befriend their children. So where does the answer lie? Let's take a look at a common scenario that happens to parents whether their teenagers are at risk or not.

You come home from a long day of work or have had a stressful day at home with your younger children. Your teenager comes home and tells you that she failed a test, and you know she didn't do her homework. She also refuses to help you with laundry and tells you she is going directly to her room to play video games. To make the situation worse, she's rude and doesn't want to talk to you. So you start yelling at her, saying, "What's wrong with you? Why don't you prepare for your tests? Look, no more video games, no more allowance . . . no more fun until you get your life together!"

Does this sound familiar? Look back at a time like this when you lost your temper, and ask yourself if your yelling made a difference or if it was just a way of discharging your frustration and anger.

In general, the value of discipline can be measured only against the backdrop of the total parent-teenager relationship. If, for example, a parent is focused on a child's inner needs and the discipline is carefully measured, then it may have a chance to affect the child in a positive way. If, however, discipline is a product of a parent's frustration or embarrassment, then a teenager will immediately sense that the parent is merely releasing anger.

The relationship is always the key to wielding indirect control on a teenager at risk.

Discipline, therefore, can be used only in direct proportion to the strength and quality of the relationship. If a parent has invested in developing the relationship with a teenager, then when discipline is needed, the child will view it as an extension of the parent's love and concern. If, however, a parent hasn't taken the time to invest in the relationship, then discipline is like throwing gasoline onto a burning flame of juvenile anger and disappointment.

Parents who are continually fighting with their teenagers about their behavior can feel as if they are on a conveyor belt that never stops moving. To change that situation, I suggest shifting parenting into "relationship mode" and creating a supportive environment in which teenagers are able "to explore their experiences openly and to reach resolution of their own problems."[3]

Let's see how this worked in the case of a boy whose parents were fighting with him about how he dressed.

Moti Wears Street Clothes

I once received a call from a distraught mother named Nechama, whose seventeen-year-old son Moti had changed his style of dress, wearing jeans and refusing to wear a hat. Her son, she explained, had gone through a difficult time in school and was now hanging around the house instead of studying in yeshiva. He was also mixed up in the wrong crowd in the neighborhood and was associating with these at-risk teenagers late at night on the street. Nechama seemed very concerned since she had an older son who had also gone "off the path" and was worried that Moti was going in the same direction. She believed that Moti could be helped if he would be willing to talk with someone.

I asked Nechama to make an appointment for her son. I knew there was a chance that he would feel pressured to come in to speak with me, so I told her that if he didn't show up, I would understand. As it happened, Moti did show up on time and seemed receptive to speaking with me in a friendly and open manner. What follows is a transcript of our meeting.

> *DS:* Moti, I know that your parents are concerned about you and they wanted you to speak with me. I just want you to know that I'm very interested to hear

what you have to say. Tell me what's going on in your life.

Moti: Well, I guess my mother told you that I hate school and I'm looking for a job.

DS: What kind of job?

Moti: It doesn't really matter. Perhaps something in business or high tech.

DS: High tech. Do you have any computer skills that would help you?

Moti: Yes, I love computers and I know how to create Web sites.

DS: That's a great skill. Did you take a class in HTML or figure it out by yourself?

Moti: I just figured it out by myself.

DS: Wow! I wish I could do that. Well, if you are so talented working with computers, why are you having so much trouble in school?

Moti: I hate my school. I can't stand the teachers and the principal.

DS: You hate your teachers?

Moti: Yes. I can't stand them. They are boring and mean and my *rebbe* doesn't know what he is talking about.

DS: You don't like your rebbe. Let me ask you a question. If you did like your rebbe, would school be any better for you?

Moti: I guess so. But there is no way he can change. Everybody knows he's the worst rebbe in the grade. He doesn't care about me. In fact he kicked me out of class twice this year.

DS: So that's why you're at home right now?

Moti: That's right.

DS: Tell me about your home. I know you have a big family. What is your relationship like with your parents?

Moti: It's pretty bad.

DS: What do you mean, bad?

Moti: My parents make me crazy.

DS: Anyone in particular?

Moti: Yes, my mother; she is always trying to control me.

DS: In what way?

Moti: She can't stand my music or the way I dress. She also hates my friends and recently made my curfew at eleven o'clock. It's unbearable to be around her.

DS: So dress is a big issue in the family?

Moti: Yes. They want to tell us what to do all the time. I feel like I'm living in a cage.

At this point, we had brought to the forefront several key issues. One was that Moti didn't like his rebbe, and another was that he felt that his parents wanted to control everything he did. At the same time, it seemed that Moti also had a very high desire for control. When he was unhappy with a situation, he would try to control his environment by making choices that elicited a negative response from his parents or teachers.

I felt that Moti was able to become aware of the dynamics of his own inner world. In his case, I believed that more self-awareness would help him understand why he behaved the way he did.

    DS: Moti, tell me about some of the things that your parents and you argue about, like your friends and your clothes.

    Moti: I don't see what's wrong with my clothes. I'm just more comfortable wearing jeans and these shirts. I mean, I don't know what the problem is, but my mother is always telling me how to dress.

    DS: Did you always dress like this? When did you start?

    Moti: Just after my bar mitzvah.

    DS: So just when you became a "man," you started dressing the way you wanted to.

    Moti: That's right.

    DS: Tell me what you think your clothing represents. Do your clothes say something about you when you wear them?

    Moti: I think so. They are all about doing what you want. When I wear jeans, I feel comfortable, more chilled out. I know it drives my parents crazy, but I love the feeling.

    DS: Do your friends wear the same type of clothes?

    Moti: Yes, we all do.

    DS: Let me guess about something and tell me if I'm right. Your clothing represents your being independent from your parents. What I mean by that is that they can't tell you how to dress and of course you can't stand how they try to control you. Does this make sense?

Moti: Yes, very much so.

DS: So what you are really saying is that this is an area that you can control and it probably makes your parents crazy.

Moti: That's right. I really dress this way because it makes them crazy. I know the weirder I dress the more it makes my mother nuts.

DS: So your dress is a way to control her.

Moti: I guess so.

DS: If you can see what I'm saying, then I want to share with you the idea that what seems to be an area of control is really an area where you are out of control. What I mean by that is that although you think you control your mother through your dress, what you are really saying is that she controls you. If you are just reacting to her and getting her more angry at you, then you are not really in control.

I knew that this idea would be hard to swallow. Especially for a boy who initially saw his jeans as something "cool" and modern. What I wanted to do was to have him understand that this alternative way of dressing was actually based on a deeper emotional need to control and confront his mother. Once I introduced this idea, I could spend more time helping him to improve his relationship with her instead of becoming more reactionary. I decided to introduce Moti to his mother's inner world. I wanted to explore with him any possible reason why she was so controlling.

DS: Tell me a little more about your mother. Does she come from a big family? What are her parents like?

Moti: Well, that's a pretty bad story. She has a terrible relationship with her parents.

DS: What do you mean?

Moti: Her parents are originally from France. They moved to Israel when she was a young girl and got divorced, and my mother moved here with my grandmother when she was a teenager.

DS: What about her brothers and sisters?

Moti: Two of them moved here with her and the others stayed with my grandfather in Israel.

DS: How did your grandmother survive here?

Moti: Well, she had a sister who moved here many years ago who helped her out a lot when she arrived.

DS: So your mother grew up without her father. That must have been pretty hard.

Moti: Yes, but it was probably easier than living with my grandfather. I heard he was pretty tough with his kids. You know, very old school. He used to hit his kids a lot.

DS: He used to hit them?

Moti: He was a tough man who had a hard life. He didn't have patience for my mother or her brothers and sisters.

DS: So your mother moved around a lot and had a hard childhood.

Moti: I think so.

DS: And what about your father. Did he also have a difficult childhood?

Moti: I don't think so. He grew up in the neighborhood, went to yeshiva, went into business, and has an okay relationship with his parents.

DS: So it seems that your mother had a harder time growing up.

Moti: Yes I think so.

DS: Would you say that your mother is a tense person?

Moti: Yes, she always walks around nervous, like something bad is going to happen.

DS: I see. So how does that make you feel?

Moti: I can't stand being around her!

DS: Are you angry that she doesn't give you enough attention?

Moti: It makes me crazy. She doesn't pay any attention to me except when she doesn't like something.

DS: Like the way you dress?

Moti: Yes.

I wanted Moti to make the connection that somehow his mother was affected by her unresolved feelings that existed in her inner world. Also, without too much information from Moti, I saw that his mother was obviously someone who had trouble relating to her children and found it difficult to nurture them in a loving way.

Throughout this first session, I had begun to uncover a deep association between Moti's behavior and his mother's emotions. In future sessions, we would deal more with trying to understand why his mother was tense and nagging. I believed that it was time for him to explore the connection with his mother and for us to see if we could work out a way to improve their relationship.

I explained to Moti that since his mother had come from a broken home and had moved several times during her childhood, she was compensating for her feelings of rejection and lack of security. This was understandable, considering her past, and it was something that I felt was central to Moti's situation. I believed that his mother was so scared of the possibility that her children's lives would be disrupted—as hers had been during her childhood—that her fears controlled her life. Moti's older brother had already decided to go on his own path. She saw this as a sign that the whole family might fall apart, and the fact that Moti was having trouble in school and dressing in jeans began to cause her considerable stress and anxiety.

I wanted Moti to understand these underlying issues and to realize why he was unhappy with their relationship. Her desire that "life should be perfect" had caused her to act overly harsh with her children, which made them feel that somehow they were not living up to her expectations. After all, Moti was a teenager trying something that his friends thought was cool. He wanted to be accepted by his crowd and knew how his behavior would affect his parents.

Having explored other emotional issues in his family, I suggested that Moti try to reduce the conflict regarding his alternative dress by toning down what he wore. I knew that his parents wouldn't easily change their expectations, but Moti could benefit from an improved relationship, and a small gesture on his part might make his life at home more pleasant.

I also spoke several times on the phone with Moti's parents and suggested that they were not yet equipped to discipline Moti about his jeans. Rather, they should work to improve the relationship and allow a new sense of closeness to eventually enable Moti to feel more comfortable with himself and his identity. They could accomplish this by

1. Reducing their criticism of Moti
2. Finding ways to give Moti healthy levels of control
3. Exploring ways of nurturing Moti's latent talents

To start the process, I suggested that Moti's parents take him away for the weekend in the country and have a fun time sightseeing, hiking, or maybe even going to a batting cage or playing miniature golf. I wanted Moti to feel comfortable with his parents. They should give Moti the feeling that he was the most important person in their lives.

During the outing, Moti's parents should avoid talking about his jeans. Rather, they should focus on his positive qualities and what areas he could potentially excel in, like music, art, computers, or even some type of community service. With an increased sense of relationship, Moti might be willing to adjust his behavior and take steps to reconnect to his family's traditions.

Trying to force the dress issue would only push their son further away. Instead of pushing him away, they could gently pull him in the right direction. In the end, we were able to change the focus from direct control and conflict to mutual understanding and an improved relationship.

MENTORING

In Moti's case, both he and his parents were willing to meet with me and then take steps to improve their relationship with one another. When the parent-teen relationship is strained or just needs improvement, parents can also use other forms of outside help to bring about change. When necessary, one of the most effective ways of wielding indirect control is by having the teenager meet with a mentor. As a person uninvolved in family conflicts, a mentor is able to interact with a teenager and provide an informal means of solving problems at school, help with doing homework, or simply friendship.

Many possibilities exist for people who can play the role of mentor. A mentor can be an older student in your child's school, someone you know in the community, a cousin or older sibling, or a youth worker from your synagogue. Often a good mentor for your teenager may be your best friend or someone that you know and admire at work.

Mentors can perform any number of functions in a teenager's life. Yet all mentors have one thing in common: they care about helping young people achieve their potential and discover their strengths. Their main purpose is to help young people define and achieve their own goals. And those goals will vary depending on the young person's age. By sharing fun activities and exposing a teenager to new experiences, a mentor encourages positive choices, promotes self-esteem, supports academic achievement, and introduces the child to new ideas.

Here are some of the roles a mentor does and does not play:
A mentor is
- A friend
- A coach

- A motivator
- A companion
- A supporter
- An advisor
- An advocate

A mentor is not

- An ATM
- A social worker
- A parent
- A cool peer
- A nag
- A parole officer
- A savior

The goal of the mentor may be to do homework with the teenager, to learn a new hobby, or just to have a good time. Most importantly, a mentor can provide quality time and instill important values, such as trust, friendship, community, and responsibility, without impinging on a teen's sense of freedom.

Unquestionably, mentors make a lasting impression on the lives of children and teenagers. Research confirms what previously we had known anecdotally or intuitively: that mentoring works. A recent research brief published by Child Trends found that "youth who participate in mentoring relationships experience a number of positive benefits."[4] In terms of educational achievement, mentored youth have better attendance, a better chance of going on to higher education, and better attitudes toward school. In terms of health and safety, mentoring appears to help prevent substance abuse and reduce some other negative behaviors. In terms of social and emotional development, mentoring promotes positive social attitudes and relationships. Mentored youth tend to trust their parents more and communicate better with them. They also feel that they get more emotional support from their friends than do youth who are not mentored.

The most compelling evidence of the impact of mentoring was found by a private study that demonstrated that compared to young people not participating in the Big Brothers, Big Sisters program, teenagers that are mentored are

- 46 percent less likely to begin using illegal drugs
- 27 percent less likely to begin using alcohol
- 52 percent less likely to skip school
- 37 percent less likely to skip class
- More confident in their schoolwork performance
- Able to get along better with their families[5]

With all this evidence taken into consideration, Relationship Theory teaches that when parents have an unusual amount of difficulty relating to their teen, finding a mentor may be one of the best routes to take.

Sometimes other people are better at telling your children truths and ideas that you find difficult to express. For example, a friend of mine has always used mentors or other third parties to impress upon his children the importance of values such as honesty, integrity, and religiosity. To do this, he invites guests to his home who have a positive effect on his children's moral development. He engages his guests in discussions about Torah learning, personal integrity, or community involvement. During these interchanges, his children pick up important and lasting messages that they can easily absorb without feeling that their parents are forcing their values upon them.

In addition to having guests, this seasoned parent always strives to arrange learning sessions with mentors or well-known rabbis for his children during their vacations. By effectively limiting his own direct control, he has more impact on his children's lives.

In addition, mentoring reduces stress between parents and teenagers. Take Sarah for example, a mother of three daughters ages nine, twelve, and sixteen. Sarah came to talk to me about her oldest daughter, Leah, who was having trouble in school.

This is how she described her problems:

> Every night we fight about her homework and I'm left with a throbbing headache. When my husband comes home, sometimes at eight or nine o'clock, depending on his busy schedule, he tries to do homework with her, but most of the time they just end up fighting over silly things. She finds it impossible to sit down and concentrate on her schoolwork for more than five minutes. She was tested for ADHD, and she doesn't have it. My daughter and I are growing further apart. Imagine if all you did was fight with someone day and night without a break.

I suggested to Sarah that trying to control her daughter wasn't working. She needed to replace direct control with indirect control and to hire a mentor to help her daughter do her homework.

To implement indirect control, Sarah also needed to
1. Avoid confronting Leah about homework.
2. Do some research with Leah's teachers to find out exactly what her problems were in class.
3. Find opportunities for her husband and her to spend quality and enjoyable time with Leah.

Sarah decided to step back and stop trying to control her daughter and shift toward a relationship-oriented style of parenting. By arranging for a tutor, she let a third person help her daughter to do better in school. She was able to move from direct control to indirect control and make a difference in Leah's life.

After a few months of tutoring, the tension in Sarah and Leah's relationship had been reduced. Leah was getting the help she needed, which was something her mother couldn't provide for her. Now when she arrived home at night after a long day's work, Sarah could focus her energy on relating better to her daughter and spending quality time with her. By shifting from direct to indirect control, Sarah enabled herself and her daughter to become closer and enjoy the benefits of a warmer and more intimate relationship.

Chaim Gives Up Religion

Let's look at an example of how mentoring improved the life of a teenager who had given up observing Jewish tradition.

Last year, two parents, Levy and Sarah, came to talk to me about their sixteen-year-old son named Chaim. These parents are first-generation Americans whose families came from Russia in the 1950s. Their family had never experienced the problem of an at-risk teenager, and they wanted to see if I could help them.

After exploring their relationship with Chaim, I wanted to find out about other relationships that may prove useful in helping Chaim to feel better about himself.

> *DS:* I realize that Chaim seems very unhappy at home. Is there anybody outside of the family that he connects with?
>
> *Sarah:* He loves going to our neighbor's house. They have a son the same age. He is a much better boy

and likes talking to Chaim. I think his parents can handle my son's *mishugas*, and Chaim likes the attitude in their home.

DS: He likes their attitude? What do you mean?

Levy: Well, they treat him differently from the way we do. You know what it's like—it's hardest to get along with the people closest to you. When you are not that close, you can be friendly.

Sarah: Probably because your friends aren't responsible for you. So whatever goes is okay.

DS: Yes, I think that's part of it. There is another reason why sometimes children prefer their friends more than their family. The reason is that their friends don't try to control or criticize them. It's like grandparents. I often say that they get all the *nachas* and none of the *tzuris*. Perhaps parents should be more like grandparents. Do you see what I mean?

Sarah: Are you saying we aren't friendly enough with him? How can we be? He is falling apart and needs help. Can't *you* do something?

DS: Well, that's what I'm here for. I try to help people realize that even in the worst cases, there is always something you can do. The first thing I want you to realize is that everything you tried up until now hasn't worked. If you want to help Chaim, you need to stop trying to control him and replace control with a deepening relationship. From the time he was born, your relationship has been based on control. You expected him to do what you wanted: when to go to bed, whom to play with, and when to do his homework. However,

> Chaim has changed; he no longer accepts your control and has taken you out of his inner world. He wants something new that you need to give him.

Sarah: What's that?

DS: He needs love and friendship. That means that you need to develop a new strategy for parenting. The more you try to control him, the further he wants to get away. I want you to end that kind of relationship and start something new.

We talked about the importance of taking all language of control and criticism out of their dialogue and replacing it with love and acceptance, and I explained the need for them to monitor their words to evaluate if they are bringing them closer or further away from Chaim.

The next week, Sarah and her husband came back for a second session. This time they seemed more optimistic. We talked about their interactions with Chaim, and they said that although nothing really changed, at least they had stopped fighting.

I was encouraged by these small steps, and I asked if Chaim would agree to come in to talk. I wanted to find out more about his inner world. Two weeks later, Chaim came into my office. Our conversation follows.

DS: Tell me a bit about what you do like in life. What are you good at in school?

Chaim: Well, I don't like studying Gemara or Chumash very much, but I do like writing and music.

DS: What do you like writing about?

Chaim: I don't know. I guess about a lot of things. I enjoy writing about outer space.

DS: What about outer space? Is it about planets, stars, or people traveling there?

Chaim: I think people going away to different galaxies is cool. They get to find out about new things and get away from this boring world. No more fighting, just finding out about new stuff.

DS: What do you think happens when people are flying in the same spaceship for a long time? Doesn't it get boring up there too?

Chaim: I guess so.

DS: So what do you think makes it interesting when you're put together in a box and are drifting out into space for years at a time?

Chaim: I'm not sure.

DS: It might be that if the people have good relationships, they probably enjoy spending a lot of time together—even out in space. Do you see what I mean?

Chaim: I guess so.

DS: What I'm trying to say is that enjoying life out in space and maybe here in this world is all about having good relationships. Can I ask you a question? What relationships do you enjoy and which people are you having trouble with?

Chaim: Well, I hate my parents and I think my rabbis are boring. I don't think I like talking to anyone. My rabbis don't have any idea how I'm feeling!

DS: Is that true? Was there a time when you knew some rabbis that you liked?

Chaim: I loved my second grade rebbe. He was really cool. I remember him talking about space. When I was in his grade, there was a launch of the space shuttle, and I remember him talking about it. He was so funny. He always knew how to get us interested in what we were learning even if he had to go off the page for a few minutes. We trusted him. He knew how to enjoy life.

At that session, I found what I was looking for—a small opening to Chaim's inner world. He was sharing with me something he had hidden away for about ten years, the rebbe he enjoyed in school. I believed that if he could connect with someone like his rebbe, he could develop a relationship that could provide a springboard for his recovery. I told Chaim that his rebbe sounded like a man he could be honest with. I asked if he would call up his rebbe and just say hello and tell him that he still had fond memories of his class. Chaim turned out to be very receptive to the idea.

Later that week, he contacted his former rebbe, who suggested that he come to meet and talk about how he was feeling. He also told Chaim that he was willing to talk to him whenever he needed and invited him to his home for a Shabbos meal.

Over the course of the next few months, despite all of the ups and downs, I saw Chaim slowly come back to life. We had numerous discussions about astronomy and space travel and about deepening his ability to maintain positive relationships with his rebbe and with his parents.

I also worked with Chaim's parents, encouraging them to follow my lead and to
1. Talk with Chaim about his interests in outer space and technology.
2. Take Chaim on a trip to the local planetarium and have a relaxing time together.
3. Reduce criticism of Chaim's behavior.
4. Find other positive role models that could help Chaim and arrange for him to spend quality time with them.

Little by little, their relationship with Chaim began to improve. Eventually, he began to participate in the Shabbos meal and even asked his father to study the *parsha* with him on Shabbos night.

Although we encountered many obstacles along the way, through finding out about Chaim's interests, working with his family to understand his inner world, and helping him renew old friendships, Relationship Theory and mentoring helped his parents reconnect to Chaim and allowed him to renew his trust and faith in their relationship and in their traditions.

Chaim began to find that his present family situation could be more gratifying than he had imagined. He and his family had implemented the principles of Relationship Theory and were now heading toward a new future together.

PARENTING TIPS

- Shift from direct control to indirect control or influence.
- Avoid confrontation.
- Realize that discipline is more effective when you combine it with working to deepen your relationship with your teenager.
- Influence your teenager's development through introducing him or her to healthy role models and mentors.

4: The Three *C*s of Relationship Theory: Communication

© 1997 Randy Glasbergen. www.glasbergen.com

GLASBERGEN

"You always complain that I don't know how to show my emotions, so I made these signs."

For both parents and teenagers alike, adolescence can be a very hard time. Unfortunately, when family life gets rough, communication tends to break down. And when it does, parents need to restore their ability to relate to their teenagers by learning about the rules of communication.

Without question, parents find it hard to deal with teenagers who are unpleasant to talk to or who limit their communication to grunts or short answers that stop abruptly at "yes" or "no."

One of the most difficult scenarios of a breakdown in communication I have ever seen was between a twelfth-grade student named Rachel and her parents. When Rachel came home after school and walked through the door, terror entered with her. Her parents explained to me that Rachel often avoided communicating with them altogether, but when she did speak, she was insulting and would respond rudely to innocent questions such as "How was your day?" or "What would you like for dinner?" This pattern of behavior would enrage Rachel's parents so much that they found themselves constantly screaming at and insulting their daughter. Unfortunately, the situation got so bad that lately Rachel was staying in her room, locking her door, and screaming at her parents when they tried to enter.

When I first saw Rachel's parents, they were very pessimistic about their daughter's future. For years, they had tried to calm her anger by buying her presents and clothing. They even offered her rewards just for talking to them, but nothing seemed to work.

Clearly, this serious communication problem needed to be resolved. After finding out more about Rachel's background and relationships, I began to speak to Rachel's parents about some of the key principles of relationships, and I suggested that they begin to practice an element of communication, as illustrated in figure 5, the Ten Commandments of Communication.

THE TEN COMMANDMENTS OF COMMUNICATION

Although they are not etched in stone, the Ten Commandments of Communication form the basis of relationship-centered communication with a teenager.

This is how it works. On one tablet are five "Thou Shalt Nots," and on the other tablet, five "Thou Shalts." Both sides are equally important. The Thou Shalt Nots represent the

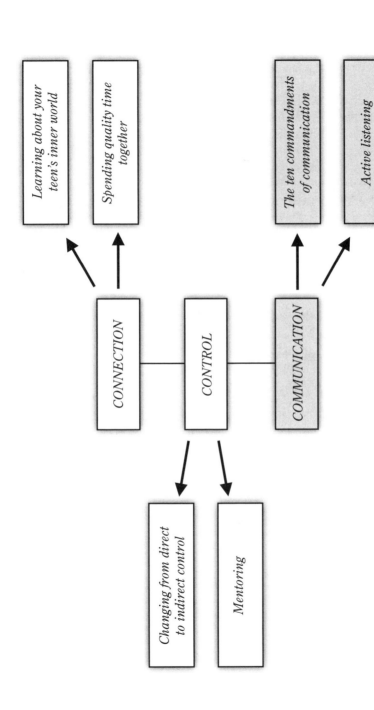

Fig. 5 The Three Cs of Relationship Theory: Communication

types of words that tend to destroy a relationship, whereas the Thou Shalts can improve the relationship and bring teenagers and parents closer together.

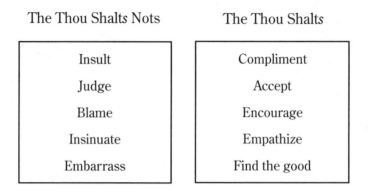

The Thou Shalts Nots	The Thou Shalts
Insult	Compliment
Judge	Accept
Blame	Encourage
Insinuate	Empathize
Embarrass	Find the good

Fig. 6. The Ten Commandments of Communication

In Rachel's case, I suggested that her parents work very hard to not use the Thou Shalt Nots. When they talked to Rachel, they needed to avoid all forms of criticism and control. The goal was to bring Rachel closer and not push her away through negative language. Although their daughter might be insulting and might often use the Thou Shalt Nots, Rachel's parents should not respond in kind. Rather, they should focus primarily on the Thou Shalts and try to empathize with her.

It's a fact of life that the Thou Shalt Nots are bound to distance people from one another. No one enjoys being criticized, blamed, or belittled for his or her behavior. Worse, parents who rely on pressure tactics to force their teenagers to change often create a negative environment that breeds more mistrust and anger in their teens. However, when parents follow the Thou Shalts and use words that are caring and compassionate, they *can* create a warmer and friendlier relationship.

Take a moment to review your relationship with your teenager. Are your words accepting, friendly, compassionate, and understanding? Or are they critical, aggressive, insulting, or belittling?

By looking at figure 6, you can evaluate whether you are transgressing the Thou Shalt Nots or fulfilling the Thou Shalts of communication. If the content and tone of the conversations you are having are angry, critical, and confrontational, then it's up to you to move over to the positive commandments and to improve the tone and content of your words. I would suggest that the ratio of positive to negative words should always remain four to one. As we learned earlier, the relationship parents can build is like a wise investment. Each positive word is one more coin in the parents' emotional savings account with their teenager.

Also, always measure your words before they are spoken. Strive to convey this positive *inner* message: "I love you and care about you, and I want to deepen our relationship," and evaluate whether what you are about to say will push your child further away or bring him or her closer.

For about two months, I worked with Rachel's family to reduce their use of criticism and compliment Rachel whenever they had a chance. At first, changing their style of communication seemed awkward to them, but slowly they began to see that without criticism, Rachel was more willing to talk. But in their case, I believed that they needed to go even further. Knowing how intense the conflict between them was, I also suggested that they go on an "emotional diet," based on the "Emotional Food Pyramid," to help them develop a better form of communication.

The Emotional Food Pyramid

The original Food Pyramid was designed as an easy way to show people what groups of foods they needed to eat to be healthy. Its pyramid shape (rather than a circle or square) helps explain which foods you should eat more or less of. The foods that make up the pyramid's base (the widest part) should provide the biggest part of your diet. As you move up the pyramid, the amounts of different foods you need get smaller.

In the same way, families having trouble maintaining a positive relationship with their teenagers should follow the Emotional Food Pyramid shown in figure 7. To begin with, a healthy emotional diet must be based heavily on large amounts of compassion and understanding, including at least five or six portions of kind and loving words daily.

As a parent progresses to the next level of the pyramid, some words of indirect control may be used in moderation. For example, phrases like "Let's try to work this out together" or "Are you sure you can handle that alone?" are appropriate in small amounts. The most important dynamic of communication is always to lean toward the positive and use fewer words of control.

If a parent needs to criticize a teenager, this should be done very carefully. Criticism can be viewed as a kind of emotional cholesterol that blocks the flow of positive communication and damages the relationship. Similar to a person who is at high risk for heart disease and who needs to avoid cholesterol, when a teenager is at risk, parents need to avoid all forms of emotional cholesterol as much as possible. Being extra careful with criticism is a sure-fire way of reducing bad feelings in the relationship.

Remember that the diet can change based on the quality of the relationship. For instance, if the relationship between parents and teens is severely strained, then parents need to take extreme caution to avoid all forms of criticism. If the relationship improves, then parents can start using some servings of indirect control.

Fig. 7 The Emotional Food Pyramid

Following a diet isn't always easy, but the benefits can last a lifetime. Parents who follow the advice reflected by the Emotional Food Pyramid may find that in the long run, they are able to sustain meaningful relationships with their teenagers and avoid the common pitfalls of dealing with at-risk behavior.

Some parents get used to constant friction in their relationship with their teenagers and are always caught up in a power struggle. By following the Emotional Food Pyramid, Rachel's parents were able to move out of such a struggle, free up positive emotional energy, and allow their daughter the space she needed to feel secure in their new relationship.

I urge parents in Rachel's parents' situation to take the first step toward improving communication. I know how hard that may be, but I believe that when one person makes a change and starts to practice the Thou Shalts of the Ten Commandments of Communication, the other person eventually notices a difference in tone and attitude and responds in kind. It may take some time to see a positive change—even weeks or months—but those who follow these rules can reap the long-term benefits of a closer and more pleasant relationship. Once the basic rules are followed, parents can focus on a higher level of communication called *active listening*.

ACTIVE LISTENING

When parents hear that they need to improve their communication skills, they often think that this advice refers to talking. But in actuality, talking is only one part of communication. The other important component of communication is being able to listen.

Let's try to understand the power of parents who are able to actively listen to what their teenagers are saying. To begin with, it's helpful for parents to think about what it feels like when others listen to them. Imagine you had someone who always listened to you in a loving and empathetic way. Most people would even be willing to pay money to have someone listen to their feelings about issues like their job, spouse, or children. In fact, many people do pay psychologists and psychiatrists large sums of money in order to have someone listen to and validate their feelings.

In the same way, for parents looking to improve communication with their children, active listening is a powerful technique that gives teenagers a sense that they can safely express their feelings without fear of criticism.

The Goal of Communication

When parents speak to their teenagers, two misconceptions are usually floating in their minds:

- My teen is speaking to me because he or she wants something.
- The purpose of my speaking to my teen is to correct his or her behavior.

I'm not denying that most teenagers—or for that matter most children—speak to their parents because they want something. Most people communicate with others to achieve certain goals, such as acquiring possessions, making money, attaining valuable services, and so on. Communication is therefore seen as a way that people get what they want. To some extent, this is also true of teenagers. They are probably coming to their parents for money, advice on how to deal with a teacher in school, suggestions for handling problems with their siblings, or similar assistance. With this in mind, a parent may feel on guard and defensive about several areas, including their money, their reputation, and their possible feelings of guilt that they can't solve all their children's problems.

The second misconception is that whatever information parents are about to receive from their teenagers somehow needs to be critiqued. It's one of the reasons that parents often feel on guard. The train of thought is "if they are telling me something, I need to tell them to do something about it."

Based on these two misconceptions, parents assume that the purposes of communicating with their teenagers are (1) to service their needs and (2) to correct their behavior. In this kind of emotional environment, healthy communication is stymied since both sides have expectations and a mistaken understanding of the purpose of communicating. Also, parents who live with these misconceptions often develop negative patterns of communication, as the following examples present.

- *The Judge.* Judges think that their teens are coming in front of a court to be judged. They commonly say things like
  - "You were wrong!"
  - "It's your fault!"
  - "You should have known better!"
- *The Psychologist.* Psychologists believe that their teenagers are harboring unresolved emotional issues that are inhibiting positive performance. They often make statements like
  - "I guess you are still angry at your father and that's why you got in a fight today."
  - "Stop feeling so bad about yourself."
  - "You're having trouble making friends because you are so introverted."
- *The Healer.* Healers may say things like
  - "Don't worry; everything will be okay."
  - "Tomorrow will be better."
  - "You should think about all the good things that happened to you today."
- *The Shrugger.* Shruggers say things like
  - "So what?"
  - "It's not important."
  - "Forget about it."

So what is the right attitude that can help parents improve their relationships with their teenagers? Is there a way to communicate that endears teenagers to their parents and creates a positive emotional environment?

According to Relationship Theory, the way to become a better communicator is to become a better listener. Parents can begin this transition by becoming aware of the goal of positive communication. Simply put, the purpose of communication is to allow the other person to feel that someone cares and is interested in actively listening to whatever emotions that person is experiencing, whether they relate to failure in school, difficulty with peers, or sibling rivalries.

Techniques for Active Listening

Instead of communication coming to a standstill, conversations between parents and teens need to go further than before. Opinions and feelings need to be shared, and parents' ability to really listen to their teen's message can go a long way in showing the teen that they care. As Dr. Chaim Ginott writes in *Between Parent and Child: The Bestselling Classic That Revolutionized Parent-Child Communication*, "Such responses create intimacy between parent and child. When children feel understood their love for the parent is deepened. A parent's sympathy is emotional first aid for bruised feelings."[1]

Here are the three most important ways to actively listen to a teenager:

1. Listen attentively and do not try to finish the teenager's sentences.
2. Acknowledge the teenager's feelings.
3. Restate what the teenager says to you.

In applying these three active listening techniques, the following key elements are appropriate:

Be patient. Parents are often tempted to speak before listening to what teenagers have to say. Teens may take some time to find the right words. Allow teenagers to express themselves, and listen patiently while they talk.

Avoid dead-end questions. Try to ask questions that will extend interaction rather than cut it off. Questions that require a yes or no answer lead a conversation to a dead end. The best approach is to ask questions that encourage teenagers to describe, explain, or share their ideas.

Know when to stop. Watch for signals that it's time to end a conversation. When teenagers start getting silly, stare into space, or simply stop responding, parents should probably stop talking and resume the conversation another time.

Hear the feelings behind words. Behind every word is a feeling that may not be apparent at first. To help teenagers get in touch with the feelings behind their words, parents should be attentive to both the words and the body expressions that signal what is going on below the surface. Good active listeners are able to help teenagers identify their feelings and allow them to express their thoughts without being judged or criticized. Here are some of the ways your teenager may be feeling:

- Angry, irritated, hostile, annoyed
- Depressed, disappointed, ashamed, powerful, guilty
- Upset, indecisive, embarrassed, hesitant, shy
- Helpless, alone, fatigued, inferior, useless
- Afraid, fearful, nervous, panicky, restless, anxious
- Hurt, dejected, rejected, offended, deprived
- Sad, anguished, desperate, pessimistic, unhappy, lonely

Equipped with an awareness of your teens' possible emotions, your next step is to help your teenagers express their feelings, which you can do in the following ways:

1. Ask them to tell you what they are upset about.
2. Ask them to restate what they are bothered by in terms of how they feel about the situation.

For example, when a teenager says, "I hate my teacher," parents can respond, "What did the teacher do to make you upset?" After you identify the problem, ask the teenager to rephrase the thought in terms of feelings. If the teen finds this difficult to articulate, then parents should gently try to elicit a response by saying, "How did your teacher make you feel? Do you feel angry, ashamed, hurt, or dejected?"

Or, if teenagers come home one day and say, "I can't stand my friends who were mean to me in class today," parents can ask their teenagers to clarify what specific actions their friends took to bother them and how they are feeling about it.

By helping to identify teenagers' feelings behind their words, parents can bring to the forefront painful emotions that often remain below the surface and inhibit positive emotional growth. By gently prompting teenagers to express their emotions, parents can help them alleviate possible feelings of isolation and strengthen their trust in the relationship, assuring them that the parents will always be available to discuss whatever they may be going through.

Mirror Your Child's Feelings

One of the most important skills good listeners have is putting themselves in the shoes of others or empathize with the speaker by attempting to understand his or her thoughts and feelings. As a parent, try to mirror your teenager's feelings by repeating them. You might reflect your teenager's feelings by commenting, "It sounds as if you're angry at your math teacher." Restating or rephrasing what teenagers have said is useful when they are experiencing powerful emotions that they may not be fully aware of. The second conversation below is a great example of a parent reflecting her teenager's feelings and at the same time helping her son change the type of videos that he watches.

A common battle parents have with their teenagers is about how much time they spend watching videos or playing computer games. Let's look at two different modes of communication. In the first conversation, the parent is unable to deal with the inner needs of her thirteen-year-old child.

> *Mom:* Sam, are you watching those ridiculous videos again? It's time to turn off the television and do your homework!
>
> *Sam:* Mom, I need to watch my videos! All my friends watch this many videos in their homes!
>
> *Mom:* I don't care. You have to get your life together and stop wasting time!

Sam: Yes! Then I'll be the big loser who doesn't know what everyone else is talking about!

Mom: So what? I don't care what other kids talk about. You have to take responsibility for your own actions.

Sam: I don't care what you want. I have got to watch them.

Mom: That's it. I'm taking the video machine away!

In the following conversation, Sam's mother has learned the skills needed to be a good active listener and mirrors her son's feelings.

Mom: Sam, I'm concerned about how many videos you have been watching lately. I think we need to set up some kind of schedule to make sure you are doing your homework and other things besides watching television.

Sam: Mom, I need to watch my videos! All my friends watch this many videos in their homes!

Mom: You'll feel like you're missing out on something if you don't watch all the videos your friends watch.

Sam: Yes! Then I'll be the big loser who doesn't know what everyone else is talking about!

Mom: If you don't know what your friends are talking about, you're afraid you'll look dumb and they'll make fun of you.

Sam: Exactly, Mom! You see why I just have to watch all these videos.

> *Mom:* Hmm, I can see that videos are important to you. Why don't we talk more about what specific videos you feel you need to watch and see if we can't come up with a compromise?

Through active listening, this parent was able to avoid an argument with her son while at the same time, she negotiated with him about watching fewer videos. Practicing this kind of communication helps build a more caring relationship, one that will enable more positive interactions and dialogue on many important matters.

Empathize with Your Teenager

Finally, empathizing with your teenager may be the greatest emotional gift you can share with him or her. To empathize, parents need to listen to their children's feelings, thoughts, and desires. Here is a good example of a parent using empathy to deepen his relationship with his fifteen-year-old teenager.

> *Andrea:* Rachel's grandma died yesterday.
>
> *Dad:* I'm sure Rachel is really sad that she lost her grandma.
>
> *Andrea:* She was always so nice when we went to visit her.
>
> *Dad:* Your visits meant so much to her.
>
> *Andrea:* I can't believe she died.
>
> *Dad:* You really enjoyed knowing her.
>
> *Andrea:* I loved her so much. What will I do without her?

Dad: You loved her so much.

Andrea: When Moshiach comes, we will see her again. Right, Dad?

Dad: For sure. I love you.

Active Listening in Practice

Here are some examples of parents who are unaware of the rules of Relationship Theory contrasted with parents who are actively listening. Read carefully as the actively listening parent keeps the key principles in mind and builds a closer relationship with her sixteen-year-old teenager.

Rebeccah Is Angry. In this conversation, Rebeccah's mother is unaware of the techniques of active listening.

Rebeccah: My teacher says that she's canceling our school trip because our class isn't behaving well.

Mom: I guess it's time to start behaving better.

Rebeccah: Yeah, just because some kids don't behave, we all have to get punished!

Mom: Maybe you do.

Rebeccah: I can't believe my teacher. She is really an idiot.

Mom: Don't talk like that about your teacher.

Rebeccah: Why do we all have to suffer because of a few stupid girls?

Mom: Because you probably all behave badly.

Rebeccah: Oh, I hate school.

In this example, Rebeccah's mother uses active listening techniques.

Rebeccah: My teacher says that she's canceling our school trip because our class isn't behaving well.

Mom: That must make you really disappointed. I know you were looking forward to it.

Rebeccah: Yeah, just because some kids don't behave, we all have to get punished!

Mom: Yeah, I see.

Rebeccah: I can't believe my teacher. She is really an idiot.

Mom: Your teacher is making you feel upset.

Rebeccah: Yeah, why do we all have to suffer because of a few stupid girls?

Mom: You feel you're suffering because of some of the girls.

Rebeccah: That's right.

Notice how the active listening parent is allowing her child to speak about her feelings and not trying to solve her problems. By doing so, she is building trust and communicating to Rebeccah that she can always approach her mother when she is upset.

Steven Gets Punched. Here, the mother is not using active listening techniques with fourteen-year-old Steven.

Steven: Chaim punched me today during lunchtime.

Mom: What a jerk that kid is!

Steven: Yeah, he's an idiot.

Mom: You better believe it.

Steven: I'm going to kill him tomorrow!

Mom: Tell him never to touch you again.

Steven: I'm first going to tell the Rebbe.

Mom: Tell him how bad that kid is and that he should be punished.

Using active listening produces an entirely different conversation.

Steven: Chaim punched me today during lunchtime.

Mom: Chaim punched you.

Steven: Yeah, he's an idiot.

Mom: I see.

Steven: I'm going to kill him tomorrow!

Mom: Getting punched really hurt you.

Steven: Yeah, I'm going to tell the Rebbe.

Mom: I hear how much you want Chaim to stop punching you.

Steven: That's right.

WHAT TO DO WHEN TEENS DON'T WANT TO TALK

I once met a fourteen-year-old boy who always walked around grunting. A conversation with his parents usually sounded like this:

Mother: How was school today?

Son: Grunt.

Mother: How did you do on your test?

Son: Leave me alone.

Mother: I just want to know how things are going.

Son: Grunt.

Even the best communicators don't always succeed in having their teenagers expose their deepest feelings. At certain times, teenagers simply do not want to talk about what they are going through. And some teenagers just don't like talking about their inner world at all. When that's true, then it's best not to push too hard. It's better to try to understand why they may be feeling the way they do. Possible reasons for teens' shortened and cut-off style of communication may be that they are feeling overwhelmed, stressed, or tired or that they are just having a terrible day. Parents must realize that just because their teens are unpleasant, their children do not necessarily hate them, and they have not necessarily failed somehow. More often than not, negative behavior is a sign that teenagers are experiencing inner turmoil. Parents can help their teenagers communicate their inner feelings but only when a teenager feels comfortable to do so.

If your teenager cuts you off when you are speaking, don't try to force the issue. Once you have tried positive forms of communication, backing off is acceptable. At some point, teenagers will present their parents with further opportunities to engage in conversation, although perhaps it won't be about the subject that was originally bothering them; their feelings tend to change even on an hourly basis.

As a parent, you also should not expect yourself to be a perfect communicator. Changes will come through practice. When used thoughtfully, active listening is a very useful skill. With practice and diligence, parents can become effective listeners and establish a more positive relationship with their teenagers.

PARENTING TIPS

- Ask for comments as opposed to offering them.
- Show sincere interest in your teenager when he or she is speaking.
- Empathize with your teenager.
- Reduce criticism and negative comments.
- Use more loving and positive words when you communicate.
- Actively listen to your teenager's inner messages.
- Avoid judging or playing the role of psychologist.
- Learn when it's best not to force the issue.

5: Parents At Risk, Teens At Risk

GLASBERGEN

"This is the nicest conversation we've had in weeks.
Let's not spoil it by talking."

When parents come to talk to me about a troubled teenager, I often find it helpful to explore whether or not their marriage is causing their teenager to be at risk.

It's no coincidence that difficult marriages create difficult children. Children want their parents to be happy, and they want their parents to be together. When things are going wrong in the parents' relationship, children are often the first to sense that Mommy and Daddy are not getting along. Even if parents say that they are only arguing behind closed doors, children can still sense that something may not be right.

The parents' relationship may be one of the most important factors influencing a teenager's behavior. How parents learn to manage conflict between themselves can make a difference in their teenagers' lives. Unresolved conflict has a tremendous negative impact. It directly affects the parties themselves—the two parents involved—carrying out their normal job duties. And when parents become preoccupied with their own marital discord, teenagers can feel rejected, depressed, and isolated from their parents.

Marital conflict affects teenagers in various ways. First, conflict between the parents tends to both change the mood of household interactions and shift the parents' attention to the negative behaviors of their children. Second, parental conflict leads to parents issuing confusing and threatening commands to their children. Third, children who are exposed to harsh discipline practices at home (which tend to coincide with a negative and hostile relationship between the parents) are more at risk for aggression, internalizing by withdrawing, and depressive symptoms.

In addition, I have found that when teenagers are exposed to high levels of conflict between their parents, they don't get used to it. They become more sensitive and reactive to it, which causes many of the symptoms of at-risk behavior. Even moderate amounts of parental conflict can wreak havoc on the lives of children, disrupting their sleep and causing negative feelings in their day-to-day lives.

In many instances, parents are unaware that they might channel their anger toward their spouse through their children. This "triangling" is a very dangerous pattern of behavior that can have serious implications for children and teenagers.

Here is how triangling works. Suppose a wife is angry at her husband for not being affectionate toward her. If she is unable to express her feelings to her husband in a direct way, she may unwittingly begin to use her children to communicate to her husband her feelings of displeasure and anger. For example, she may turn to her daughter in front of her husband and say, "Oh, Daddy seems very tense today and I guess he has no time for the family." In this case, the parent is unable to negotiate her own needs and inappropriately begins to involve her child in a private marital issue.

The child who is caught in a triangle like this has become an inappropriate conduit for the expression of the mother's anger toward her husband. When this happens, children can develop feelings of disillusionment, fear, insecurity, and vulnerability. They also may feel that they have to take sides because they can't manage the internal tension and the anxiety by themselves. In these cases, they may see one parent as mostly bad and the other parent as mostly good. This is damaging to children because it reinforces an attitude by which they view the world in a "black and white" or "all or nothing" way rather than with a more balanced view of good and bad in most people.

Here are some of the signs that parents are engaged in triangling with their children:

- One parent wants the child to talk to or do something about his or her relationship with the other.
- One family member talks to the child about another and only in terms of the other's negative qualities.
- One or both parents blame the child for the problems they have with each other.
- The child believes he or she is somehow responsible for the problems between the parents.
- The child feels anxious when around certain members of the family.
- The child thinks he or she can bring peace and harmony to members of the family with enough effort.

- The child leaves family gatherings feeling tense, anxious and/or emotionally drained.[1]

Parental fighting affects children in varying ways, depending on their age. For example, teenagers around the age of fifteen or sixteen are most likely to involve themselves in their parents' battles. Younger children may keep their feelings hidden inside and may only show signs of depression in late childhood or early adolescence. Other children may adapt to parental fighting by becoming "too good." To stop the fighting, they try to become perfect children. These model children try to do everything right while walking on eggshells, fearing their family will collapse if they make a mistake.

Unfortunately, more and more children seem to be growing up in families with marital conflict. The number of divorced Americans rose from "4.3 million in 1970 to 18.3 million in 1996," and the trend is so well established that "40 percent of all children born in the 1970s and 1980s—today's teenagers and young adults—have experienced the breakup of their family through divorce."[2] To this large number, add all the children whose parents are unhappy with each other but don't divorce. It's not hard to see that a substantial segment of the population grows up in very unhappy homes.

THE EFFECTS OF DIVORCE
ON CHILDREN AND FAMILIES

Here are some effects that divorce may have on children and teenagers:

- Children whose parents have divorced are increasingly the victims of abuse and neglect. They exhibit more health problems as well as behavioral and emotional problems, are involved more frequently in crime and drug abuse, and have higher rates of suicide.

- Children of divorced parents more frequently demonstrate a diminished learning capacity, performing more poorly than their peers from intact two-parent families in reading, spelling, and math. They also are more likely to repeat a grade and to have higher drop-out rates and lower rates of college graduation.

- Divorce generally reduces the income of the child's primary household and seriously diminishes the potential of every member of the household to accumulate wealth. For families that were not poor before the divorce, the drop in income can be as much as 50 percent. Moreover, decline in income is intergenerational, since children whose parents divorce are likely to earn less as adults than children raised in intact families.

- Religious worship, which has been linked to health and happiness as well as longer marriages and better family life, is less prevalent in divorced families.[3]

Parents usually experience a lot of pain when divorced, and the most common ways of handling that pain are either to withdraw from their children or to become overprotective. Children are sensitive to their parents' feelings and have many ways of dealing with this trouble, both internally and externally. Children may respond with depression or guilt, feeling that somehow the pain is entirely their fault. Most children have a never-ending hope that their parents will reconcile, even after one or both parents have remarried. Therefore, a sense of abandonment by one or both parents is very common for such children and may contribute to at-risk behavior during adolescence.

ASSESSING YOUR MARRIAGE

Parents of a teenager at risk need to ask themselves some very pointed questions to evaluate the quality of their marriage. Some of the questions are listed here:

- Are you sensitive to your partner's needs?
- Do you argue fairly?
- Do you resolve conflicts easily?
- When you talk to each other, do you feel you have been heard? If not, why?
- Are you content with your emotional, social, and physical intimacy?
- Do you have fun together? Do you joke in a friendly way about the bad times you may be having?
- Are you forgiving with each other?
- How do you handle the division of household responsibilities?

Take a few minutes to evaluate with your spouse how you are doing in your marriage. The first step you must take is acknowledging and accepting any trouble in your marriage. It is common for people to brush off an issue, expecting it will take care of itself and eventually go away. Nobody wants marital problems, but if you ignore them, you will only be giving them room to grow. Talk to your spouse about problems and work together for a solution with which you both agree and feel comfortable.

Not all marital issues can be resolved by the couple. Some marriage problems are too sensitive to handle alone. The subjects of such problems might include unfaithfulness; sexual frustrations; conflict involving in-laws, friends, siblings, and children; verbal abuse; and so on. When parents are dealing with such problems, the best course is to ask a professional outside party for advice and opinions.

Why You Should Receive Expert Advice

Many people hesitate to receive expert advice because they are unfamiliar with it and feel uncomfortable. But professional advice is helpful and important because relationship experts have studied and dealt with similar or identical situations to yours and can assist you in seeing yours from many perspectives with several solutions, one or more of which will suit you and your marriage best.

So no matter what your marital trouble may be, always remember these important steps:

- Acknowledge and accept the problem.
- Ask yourself why the problem troubles you.
- Approach your partner with your thoughts and feelings.
- Talk it out.
- Stay rational.
- Seek an expert's opinion and advice.

If, after evaluating your marriage, you have found unresolved areas of tension, it's important to try to resolve your problems before they spill over into the life of your child or teen. Improving your marriage may be the most important thing you can do to help your teenager.

MOSHE DROPS OUT OF SCHOOL

A few years ago, a couple named Sarah and Joseph came to see me about their son Moshe, sixteen, who was experiencing extreme difficulty in school. Moshe did not have any serious learning problems. In fact, he was exceptionally bright and capable of succeeding in school. His problem was that he was frequently missing class. Recently, he had started leaving school and spending time in an unknown location. Moshe's parents were naturally concerned for his future.

When I first met Sarah and Joseph, I was immediately struck by how unhappy their marriage seemed to be. Joseph was quiet and reserved compared to his wife. Sarah seemed extremely worried about whether everything was all right with her son.

When Sarah and Joseph tried to explain to me why they thought Moshe was in trouble, the discussion always seemed to turn into an argument. Joseph believed that his wife's inability to nurture their son was the cause of Moshe's behavior. Sarah, on the other hand, believed that Joseph's inability to communicate in a warm way with their son was the source of the problem.

Here is a dialogue from one of our sessions:

DS: Tell me more about the general atmosphere in the house.

Sarah: Well, our family time is not very enjoyable. I would say that Shabbos meals are the most difficult time of our week. To start with, Joseph doesn't run a very nice Shabbos meal. He is so tired from work that when Shabbos rolls around, he goes to *shul*, makes Kiddush, and then totally withdraws into himself.

DS: Is Shabbos that hard for you?

Joseph: Look, it's not that I don't care about the family; it's just that I feel so burnt out after work. When I come home, the kids are always yelling and I just want some peace and quiet. I guess on Shabbos I just need a break.

Sarah: It's worse than that. You never have time for the kids or for me. When you're home, you just surf on the Internet, and on Shabbos you read the newspaper. Don't you realize that Moshe needs to talk to you?

110

DS: I guess things are hard during Shabbos. What about your own relationship outside of your children? How well do you get along?

Sarah: To be perfectly honest, we don't have much of a relationship. Joseph isn't very excited about talking to me and we never go on vacation anymore.

Joseph: That's not true. Last Pesach we went away to Florida for the seder meals.

Sarah: We barely talked the entire week. I think you enjoyed your friends more than you enjoyed the family.

Joseph: What do you want from me? I tried my best. I can't stand when everyone is nagging—your parents, the kids, you.

DS: Have you been having trouble relating for some time?

Sarah: Yes. I would say for about the last three years.

DS: Why? What was going on in your lives three years ago?

Sarah: Well, my husband is in computers, and after 9/11 his company started downscaling and he lost his job.

DS: What did you do?

Joseph: I was on unemployment for about four months when I found a job with another company.

DS: Are you happier now?

Joseph: Not really. It's an average job, and I don't really enjoy the work I am doing. However, it does pay the bills.

DS: That's a big burden, having to support your family doing something you don't enjoy.

Joseph: I wish I could get out of it, but it's not easy to switch at my age.

I realized that at this point I had found a small opening that perhaps would help us to explore their relationship in connection to their son's delinquency. Sarah had mentioned that her husband lost his job about three years ago. I wondered if this also had a significant impact on Moshe.

    DS: You mentioned before that the problems at work started about three years before. When did Moshe start having trouble in school?

Sarah: About two years ago.

    DS: Is it possible that some of the work stress started spilling over into Moshe's life just after Joseph lost his job?

Sarah: Maybe, but I'm not sure.

    DS: Is it possible that the strain on the family became greater after Joseph lost his job, and this is the reason that you also are not getting along so well anymore?

Sarah: It's possible. Two years ago I started working again, and since then I have been unable to give the kids the kind of attention I used to give before things got hard.

During that session, I was able to refocus their energy from solving Moshe's problem to solving their marital discord. Over the next few sessions, we began exploring the way Relationship Theory could help their marriage. We talked about spending quality time together, understanding each other's needs, and reducing critical and destructive language.

After six months of working with this family, I began to see changes in the way the parents related to their son. Moshe began to feel more comfortable in their home and was more willing to give school a try and focus on his studies.

In general, Moshe's family was typical of the families I see with teens at risk. Often, some type of emotional imbalance exists in the family, and eventually one or more children begin to exhibit signs of distress. When they do, the best approach for the parents is to seek professional advice and find ways to improve their relationships with their children.

Resolving intra-parental conflict is a positive step parents can take to help support the emotional growth of their children. A good family or marital counselor will be able to break habitual patterns of triangling and relieve the emotional distress that may be contributing to a teenager's at-risk behavior.

PARENTING TIPS

- Explore your relationship with your spouse, and check for any unresolved issues that may be affecting your teenager.
- Avoid triangling and communicating to your spouse via your teenager.
- If necessary, seek professional advice on how to improve your marriage.

6: Putting It All Together

GLASBERGEN

"Son, we need to spend more quality time together.
Stop by my office and fill out a job application."

By now we have covered many of the major ways to understand what makes a teenager tick. Now it's time to put all the pieces together and work toward restarting the relationship between you and your teenager.

Beginning again is never easy, especially when starting over demands that a person develop new habits. However, restarting a relationship with a teenager is easier than most parents think. Old habits *can* be replaced by new ones as long as you follow the Three *C*s and keep the goals of Relationship Theory in mind.

In this book, we have learned about the importance of three key areas—connection, control, and communication. Remembering them, parents can use the following techniques

to help jump-start their relationship with their teenager:
- Reframing
- Communicating intent to change
- Keeping the goals in mind

REFRAMING

Reframing can help parents view their teenager from a new perspective. Seeing the relationship from a different angle can lessen the effects of a long history of bitter emotions.

One way to reframe the entire relationship is for parents to depersonalize the conflict by viewing their teenager as a unique and separate individual. One technique I teach parents is to treat their teenager as though the teen were their friend's child and not their own. With friends and acquaintances, we are extra careful not to overstep boundaries, and we work hard to stay calm and maintain our sense of compassion. Imagine how much better parents' relationships with their teens could be if the parents would relate to them with more love, politeness, and respect.

Another way for parents to reframe the relationship is to view themselves as their teen's grandparent. Many of us have fond memories of our grandparents. I always viewed mine as a tremendous source of love and generosity, and their home was a place of kindness and acceptance. I never felt belittled or criticized by my grandparents. Perhaps grandchildren have this special relationship with their grandparents because most grandparents are not the primary providers for their grandchildren and are not responsible for discipline. Parents who are able to imagine themselves as their children's grandparents and relate to their children in a grandparent's loving way can reduce friction and give their children more of the love and kindness that they need.

A third possible way for parents to reframe the relationship with their teenagers is to view themselves more like salespeople and less like chief executive officers of a company. The shift in focus works as follows: For the first ten or eleven years as a parent, you were the CEO of your family. As CEO, you were in charge of everything—how your children dressed, what they ate, whom they played with, what they watched on television, and when they went to sleep. Just like a CEO, you decided on all policies, budgets, and staffing (babysitter) issues. You called all the shots from top to bottom.

However, when your children blossomed into teenagers, everything began to change. Instead of being the CEO of your family, your role began to change and you became a salesperson.

A salesperson is very different from the CEO. Back in the office, the CEO wants results and has invested millions of dollars in inventory and staff. The CEO has investors and a board of directors to answer to, and he or she is financially responsible for the entire company.

A salesperson, however, is out "on the floor" and is hired to convince customers of their need to buy the company's products. Successful salespeople develop sales techniques that enable them to convince the customer that spending an extra $300 on the latest stereo system (for example) is important for the customer's happiness. A salesperson must be able to close the deal and try to ensure that the customer returns to buy more products in the future.

Parents of teens at risk would do well to shift from being CEOs to being salespeople in their families. Undoubtedly, teens can be difficult customers. They develop particular tastes, desires, and feelings strengthened by a powerful sense of autonomy and independence. You know you can't force them to do what you want anymore. You may keep on trying and hoping. You may even beg them to turn out the way you want them to, but they always seem to choose what *they* deem is important. In truth, your child, who is now a teenager, has become a picky consumer, and you need to learn the skills of a salesperson.

So how are you going to sell your teenager what you want him or her to buy? Any salesperson will tell you that one of the most important rules in sales is that in order to make a deal, you have to first develop your relationship with your customer. You have to keep the customer engaged and interested in pursuing the relationship. To do this, you need to find ways to assure your customers that you are sincerely concerned about their happiness and well-being. Of course, a good salesperson knows that he or she also has to wait for the right moment to sign the deal. Salespeople need to be patient. They know that sometimes just being friendly during the first encounter is what brings customers into the store a second or third time until the deal is done.

Reinterpreting Negative Behavior

Do teenagers at risk willfully try to harm or upset their parents, or are they simply acting out their pain and pent-up frustrations? As we have learned in previous chapters, teenagers at risk are not just cranky, spoiled, or rebellious. They are dealing with serious emotional issues and are confused about their identities. Many are angry about their lack of autonomy and their inability to live life the way they see fit. During this time, parents are tempted to believe that if their teenagers would just listen to their parents, their problems would somehow go away. However, teenagers at risk have a problem that is similar to a physical disease and demands professional attention.

When children are diagnosed with serious physical illnesses, do you think their parents can rightfully blame the children and claim that they are sick because they are lazy, obnoxious, or even selfish? Will the parents fight their children in an effort to make them better? Probably not. However, somehow when parents deal with teens who have emotional difficulties, they lose perspective and live under the illusion that somehow their children could change "if they just wanted to."

Instead of dismissing their teenagers' emotions, parents need to accept the fact that an at-risk teenager has a type of disease. It's not a disease that can be identified in a laboratory or under a microscope, but it is one that can be classified as a social illness that needs the same amount of attention—if not more—as a serious physical ailment. Realizing that a teenager is suffering from an illness can reduce the feelings of anger that many parents have toward their teens. Grasping the seriousness of the situation, parents can more easily maintain a compassionate stance that helps them deal with the real problems and less with their own feelings of loss of control.

Parents who have one teenager at risk and are unsure of how to explain that teenager's behavior to the rest of their children should consider teaching the other children the idea that at-risk behavior is similar to a physical illness. They should tell the children that their sibling is suffering from an illness that needs intervention and that they can help by being patient and loving with the teen. Reading this book and becoming aware of the principles of Relationship Theory would also be helpful for some children.

COMMUNICATING THE INTENT TO CHANGE

The second technique for restoring the parent-teen relationship is for parents to verbally declare their intent to restart the relationship. To do this, parents communicate the following ideas to their teenager:

1. "I'm sorry we have had a difficult relationship over the years. I will no longer fight with you or try to control you. I would just like to have a good relationship with you."

For some parents, these words may seem hard to say, but teenagers are old enough to appreciate these words of reconciliation. Imagine that someone you have been fighting with for many years said one day, "I've been thinking a lot about our relationship, and our fighting has driven us further and further apart. How about we stop fighting and start over again? I promise not to nag, bother, and attack or criticize you anymore. I will be here only as a friend who will give you advice only when you want it." Most people would feel relieved that the battle was over and glad to have a chance to start again to build a positive connection.

Of course, words are not enough. They must be followed by action. Parents need to stick to the principles of Relationship Theory by moving to improve their connection, reduce their control, and stay within the guidelines of positive and compassionate communication.

2. "All along I was looking at you and relating to you as if you were still my little child. I now realize that you have changed. You are your own unique individual."

One of the most important needs teens at risk have is to be respected as autonomous individuals by their parents and teachers. Parents of at-risk teenagers may be waging a constant war with their teenagers, trying to stop them from asserting their own identity. Relationship Theory maintains that in order to break the stalemate, parents should tell their teenagers that they now view them as independent individuals and that they respect who the teenagers are, even if they don't always agree with their teenagers' actions.

Some parents may feel that this declaration is akin to agreeing to negative behavior. However, as we have seen throughout the book, parents no longer wield full control over their teenagers. Parents would do much better to let go and give teens their own space. In this way, recognizing teens' individuality is not a sign of weakness; rather, it is part of an overall strategy to regain momentum in the relationship.

3. "If I am unaware of difficulties or problems in your life or am somehow glossing over any, please feel free to share them with me when you feel comfortable."

Teenagers at risk feel alienated from their parents. They often believe that no one is interested in hearing about their problems. They also believe that their parents have a secret agenda to control and manipulate them. In order to moderate these feelings, parents need to tell their teenagers that they no longer have an agenda. Rather, they want to talk to them about what they are actually feeling. Teenagers need to feel that their parents are a sounding board, not people who will try to criticize or control them.

I once made this declaration to a young client who was suspicious of adults, including her parents and me. She felt that as a counselor, I was somehow an extension of her parents' authority. I said honestly, "Look, I have no agenda. My only concern is for your health and happiness. If I can do anything to make your life better, please tell me."

At the following session, I felt I was meeting a new person. All along, she had felt that her parents had sent her to me to fix her problems. Instead I was straightforward with her and told her that I was there only to help her and that I had no ulterior motive.

KEEPING THE GOALS OF RELATIONSHIP THEORY IN MIND

The third technique for restarting your relationship is to monitor and maintain the positive changes that are made. Like any other difficult task in life, applying the Three Cs of Relationship Theory takes time and practice. When the going gets rough, parents need to remind themselves of the purpose for changing their attitude toward their teenager. The goals are to

- Develop a lifelong relationship.
- Motivate without coercion.
- Open new lines of communication.
- Create an environment for long-term emotional growth.

In the long run, Relationship Theory works because motivation is easier when it's provided without coercion. Teenagers can't be pushed to change, but they may be gently pulled in the right direction. In order to do this, a parent must step back and create a safe emotional "space" where the motivation can be accomplished. This space has to be friendly, respectful, and comfortable for a teenager to exist within. It must also feel safe because safety is necessary for positive emotional growth.

Keep in mind that raising a teenager is often like being the gardener of the most beautiful garden in the world.

Successful gardeners are dedicated to their gardens and to giving them all the nutrients needed for their growth. By following the principles of Relationship Theory parents can provide the nourishment and care that their teenagers need to reach their full potential and beauty and outgrow their at-risk behavior.

COMMON PROBLEMS AND
RELATIONSHIP-BASED STRATEGIES

This book presents the case for relationship-based parenting with teenagers at risk. We have also shown that parents and teenagers have the power to rebound, heal, and even flourish in ways previously unimaginable through developing enjoyable and supportive relationships in their lives. Independent of the situations parents may be facing with their teenagers—and no matter how painful—parents *can* become catalysts for their teenagers' growth, stability, and long-term happiness when they focus on their teenagers' entire being and not merely on trying to control their behavior.

Now it's time for parents to put what they have learned into action. The principles of Relationship Theory can help address some of the key issues facing teenagers today, including problems concentrating during prayers, difficulty in school, listening to secular music, smoking, rude behavior, and alcohol and drug abuse.

It is important to note, however, that the principles do not offer black-and-white solutions for these problems; rather, they provide an overall strategy for parenting that focuses on some of the issues, often hiding below the surface, that may be the underlying causes of a teenager's at-risk behavior.

Readers are urged to follow the suggestions at the end of each section and review the lessons outlined in detail throughout this book.

Problems with Prayer

Scenario: your teenager doesn't like to pray and won't go to synagogue.

Possible inner issues: control, meaning, learning disabilities, individuality

Difficulty in prayer may be rooted in several underlying issues. One common cause is that praying in synagogue can become an issue of control, especially when teenagers feel forced to go pray with their parents and siblings. Prayer can be viewed by teenagers as another obligation or chore they *have to* perform to make their parents happy.

When teenagers find it difficult to pray, it may also point to an underlying attention disorder. Some teenagers simply have trouble concentrating for long periods and may say "I hate *shul*" or "It's boring!" when they really mean "I can't sit for a long time" or "I'm crawling out of my skin because I don't like being in group settings for a long time."

Some teenagers stop praying because they don't find prayer meaningful. And this may not be their fault. Unfortunately, our schools often neglect to teach the whys of prayer. Many teenagers have grown up learning only about the obligations of communal prayer and have not developed an appreciation for the beauty, structure, and meaning behind the words.

As alternatives to confronting teenagers on the issue of prayer, possible relationship-based strategies include

- Having your teenager assessed for attention difficulties (chapter 1).
- Studying with your teenager about the meaning and symbolism behind prayer (chapter 2).
- Empowering your teenager by offering him or her choices about where and when to pray. For instance, a different *minyan* may be more enjoyable (chapter 3).
- Spending quality time alone with your teenager instead of relating to one another only during synagogue services and at family meals (chapter 2).

Difficulty in School

Scenario: A teenager is having trouble in school and is failing in one or more subjects.

Possible inner issues: learning disabilities, control, individuality.

Few challenges are as frustrating and difficult to deal with as a teenager who is having trouble in school. Often parents become agitated when they receive a disheartening report card or a call from their teenager's principal to discuss the teen's behavior. The most important strategy parents can try to adopt in this situation is to resist the temptation to blame teachers, the school, or their teenager but rather seek out the cause of their teenager's difficulties in learning.

One possible cause for failure in school is an undetected learning disability. Teenagers who struggle with learning are especially vulnerable to feelings of depression and despair. Many experience the embarrassment, confusion, and humiliation that go hand in hand with falling behind their peers in school. Behavioral and adjustment difficulties—from isolation or withdrawal to clowning or acting out—can mask less visible signs of learning difficulties. The following signs may also be clues that an individual is experiencing difficulties with learning:

- Having difficulty paying attention.
- Hiding, losing, or avoiding schoolwork or homework.
- Being especially sensitive to criticism, mistakes, or poor grades.
- Giving up easily or appearing poorly motivated.
- Showing anger and frustration when engaged in schoolwork, homework, or similar activities.
- Having attendance problems or developing school-induced sickness.
- Avoiding schoolwork through overinvolvement in other activities.

Parents, however, can become catalysts for change when they begin to address the key issues that are affecting their teenager's performance. Relationship-based strategies include

- Having your teenager evaluated for possible learning disabilities (chapter 1).
- Hiring tutors to supplement your teenager's learning (chapter 3).
- Highlighting your teenager's positive qualities (chapter 2).
- Working with your teenager's teachers to utilize his or her unique interests and abilities (chapter 3).
- Empowering your teenager with healthy levels of control (chapter 3).

Listening to Secular Music

Scenario: your teenager likes listening to popular music on an MP3 player.

Possible inner issues: control, individuality, lack of satisfying relationships.

Music is one of the most inspirational forms of fine art. In its rhythm, melody, and variety of sounds, music transmits many exciting feelings and sensations. Its power is in its ability to penetrate straight into a person's soul and to manipulate a person's feelings. Depending on its content, music can evoke the most elevated and noble feelings or produce quite the opposite by arousing self-destructive or impulsive feelings.

Since music provides a high level of enjoyment, changing a person's listening habits is a significant challenge for parents who prefer their teenagers to listen exclusively to Jewish music. It's important for these parents not to directly confront their teenagers on this issue. Rather, the first step is to understand why their teenagers choose to listen to secular music and then to address their inner needs.

Possible issues behind religious teenagers listening to secular music include a desire to control and a need to express their individuality. The underlying message is that they can "listen to whatever they want, whenever they want it." Also, many teenagers use music to escape from painful family relationships, and they tend to turn the volume up to overwhelming levels to drown out feelings of anger, depression, and resentment.

Entering into an area as private as musical taste is difficult, but it is possible to influence what teenagers listen to.

127

Possible relationship-based strategies include

- Improving your relationship with your teenager and increasing the number of shared pleasurable experiences together (chapter 2). Going to Jewish concerts together is a great place to start.
- Encouraging your teenager's talents in music, art, or athletics and helping your teen find other ways to express his or her individuality (chapter 2).
- Empowering your teenager with healthy levels of control (chapter 3).
- Giving your teenager a monthly allowance for buying Jewish music at a local Judaica store (chapter 3).
- Becoming conversant in the latest trends in Jewish music and talking to your teenager about popular CDs (chapter 2).

Smoking

Scenario: your teenager starts smoking and you detect it by smelling it on your teen's breath or by finding packs of cigarettes in his or her room.

Possible inner issues: control, self-esteem, lack of relationships.

The attractiveness of cigarette smoking is more than just the high teenagers receive through inhaling nicotine. When teenagers smoke, they are often trying to accomplish three objectives:

1. To gain control by making their own decisions
2. To gain the social status of adults
3. To gain acceptance into a popular group of teenagers who smoke

Teenagers who smoke often believe that smoking will make them look older and that they will be treated in an adult-like way. Smoking, therefore, is a statement by teenagers that they can take control of their own lives and be independent from their parents.

Smoking is also used by teenagers as a means of achieving social acceptance. By smoking, a teenager can gain entry to a selective club of teens who are willing to take chances and make their own choices independent of what their parents want from them.

Possible relationship-based strategies include
- Empowering your teenager with healthy levels of control (chapter 3).
- Working to build your teenager's self-esteem (chapter 2).
- Highlighting and nurturing your teenager's unique qualities and talents (chapter 2).
- Arranging a meeting with a mental health professional to discuss ways of quitting smoking that may include group therapy and/or pharmaceutical drugs to help wean your teenager off cigarettes (chapter 3).

Rude Behavior

Scenario: Your teenager is rude and insulting.

Possible inner issues: control, self-esteem.

One of the most common issues facing parents with a teenager at risk is the teenager's use of rude and offensive language. Unfortunately, parents tend to fight fire with fire and respond by yelling back or confronting their teenager's rudeness. According to Relationship Theory, parents need to avoid power struggles and instead work to understand the inner issues that are motivating their teenager's behavior.

Most of the time, rude behavior is a symptom of extreme frustration. Teenagers who haven't learned how to express their needs tend to bottle up their emotions and let them loose on their parents and teachers.

Other possible causes of rude behavior include feelings of loss of control and poor self-esteem. When teenagers feel bad about their self-image, they sometimes project their feelings onto their parents by blaming them for their frustration and feelings of anger and resentment.

Instead of confronting their teenagers' behavior, it's best for parents to tell their teenagers that due to their behavior, they are unable to speak with them under the current circumstances. Then, parents should wait for an appropriate occasion when their teenager will be more open to discussing his or her inner issues in a calm and respectful manner.

Relationship-based strategies include

- Actively listening to your teenager's inner messages (chapter 4).
- Empowering your teenager with healthy levels of control (chapter 3).
- Investing in your relationship with your teenager (chapter 1).
- Highlighting and nurturing your teenager's unique qualities and talents (chapter 2).

Drug and Alcohol Use and Abuse

Scenario: you suspect that your teenager is drinking alcohol or using drugs.

Possible inner issues: control, self-esteem.

Alcoholism and drug abuse are clearly rough challenges to deal with. Yet nobody is too young (or too old) to have trouble with alcohol or drugs. That's because alcoholism and drug abuse are illnesses. They can hit anyone—including Orthodox teenagers.

But what causes certain teenagers to experiment with alcohol and drugs? As a certified alcohol and substance abuse professional, I have found that low self-esteem as well as lack of parental support, monitoring, and communication are significantly related to frequency of drinking, heavy drinking, and drunkenness among teenagers. Harsh, inconsistent discipline and hostility or a parent's rejection have also been found to significantly predict adolescent drinking and alcohol-related problems.

If you suspect alcohol or drug abuse, several relationship-based strategies include

- Working to improve your relationship with your teenager (chapter 1).
- Empowering your teenager with healthy levels of control (chapter 2).
- Working on building your teenager's sense of self-esteem (chapter 2).
- Seeking counseling (individual and/or group) and behavioral therapies that are critical components of effective treatment. In therapy, teenagers look at issues of motivation, build skills to resist drug use,

replace drug-using activities with constructive and rewarding behaviors, and improve problem-solving skills (chapter 3).

PARENTING TIPS

- Reframe the way you view your relationship with your teenager.
- When necessary, relate to your teenager more as a salesperson and less as a CEO.
- Reinterpret negative behavior by viewing it as a sign of inner turmoil.
- Discuss with your teenager how you want to change the way you communicate.
- Keep the goals of Relationship Theory in mind.
- Have your teenager evaluated for possible learning disabilities.
- Work with your teenager's teachers to utilize his or her unique interests and abilities.
- Empower your teenager with healthy levels of control.
- Actively listen to your teenager's inner messages.

Epilogue: Hope for the Future

Despite the many challenges facing families today, parents can make a difference in their children's lives. Although I have outlined a guide to parenting teenagers based on the three Cs of Relationship Theory, a fourth dimension—optimism—can help alleviate at-risk behavior.

No matter how difficult raising teenagers is, parents can gain hope in knowing that deep down inside, every human being will respond to a sincere gesture of friendship and kindness.

Parents must always hold close to their hearts the belief and the optimism that everyone—including a teenager at risk—has the potential to overcome difficult emotional challenges. Healing, however, takes time, and to successfully navigate through this difficult chapter in their lives, children may need their parents to hover nearby, ready to catch them if they fall and ready too if they choose to embrace their parents and renew the feeling of love they once shared.

I have seen many parents in counseling who felt that they were at their wits' ends with their at-risk teenagers and were not sure whom to turn to for help. I have also found that the principles of Relationship Theory were able to shed new light on their problems and give these families hope that they can always improve in one or several areas of their relationships. Quite often teenagers will detect these minute changes and will begin to view their relationships with their parents from a new perspective.

In the end, teenagers are a work in progress, and the goal of this work is to produce adults who share with their parents a lifetime of love and memories. By believing in their teenagers' potential and by following the principles of Relationship Theory, parents can give their teens a lasting emotional message that although they may be at risk, they will never be beyond reach.

Notes

FOREWORD

1. B.S. Bowden and J.M. Zeisz, "Family Meals May Prevent Teen Problems," *APA Monitor* 28 (October 8, 1997).

CHAPTER 1

1. Kristen A. Moore and others, "Parent-Teen Relationships and Interactions: Far More Positive Than Not," *Child Trends Research Brief* no. 2004–25 (2004): 2–4, http://www .childtrends.org/Files/Parent_TeenRB.pdf.Ibid.
2. I'm grateful to the following authors for helping me grasp the importance of relationship-based parenting and the psychology of Relationship Theory: John Bowley, *A Secure Base: Parent-Child Attachment and Healthy Human Development* (London: Routledge, 1988); Murray Bowen, MD, *Family Therapy in Clinical Practice* (New York: Jason Aronson, 1985); John Bradshaw, *Bradshaw On: The Family* (Deerfield Beach, FL: Health Communications, 1988); William Miller and Stephen Rollnick, *Motivational Interviewing: Preparing People for Change*, 2nd ed. (New York: Guilford Press, 2002); Salvador Minuchin, *Families and Family Therapy* (Cambridge, MA: Harvard University Press, 1974); Carl Rogers, *On Becoming a Person* (Boston: Houghton Mifflin, 1961); Walter Toman, *Family Constellation*, 3rd ed. (New York: Springer Publishing, 1976); and Rabbi Abraham J. Twerski, MD, *Positive Parenting: Developing Your Child's Potential* (Brooklyn: Mesorah Publications, 1996).

3. Alexis Harrison, "Luthar's Study on Affluent Adolescents Is National News," Teachers College, Columbia University, December 1, 2002, http://www.tc.columbia.edu/news/article.htm?id=4272.

4. Karol L. Kumpfer and others, "Family-Focused Substance Abuse Prevention: What Has Been Learned from Other Fields," *National Institute on Drug Abuse Monograph* 177 (1998): 78–102, http://www.drugabuse.gov/pdf/monographs/monograph177/078-102_Kumpfer.pdf.

5. "On Raising Teenagers," *Parade*, July 12, 1987.

6. Michael J. Bradley, *Your Teen Is Crazy—Loving Your Kid without Losing Your Mind* (Gig Harbor, WA: Harbor Press), 6–8; and J. N. Giedd and others. "Brain Development during Childhood and Adolescence: A Longitudinal MRI Study," *Nature Neuroscience* 2, no. 10, 1999; 2(10): 861–3.

7. "Learning Disabilities: Signs, Symptoms and Strategies," Learning Disabilities Association of America, 2004, http://www.ldaamerica.us/aboutld/parents/ld_basics/ld.asp.

8. Ibid.

9. "Statistics—Adolescent Depression," About Teen Depression, http://www.about-teen-depression.com/depression-statistics.html.

CHAPTER 2

1. Viktor Emil Frankl, *The Will to Meaning* (New York: Meridian, 1969, 1998), 16.

CHAPTER 3

1. William Glasser, MD, *Unhappy Teenagers: A Way for Parents and Teachers to Reach Them* (New York: HarperCollins, 2002), 12.
2. Rabbi Abraham J. Twerski, M.D, *Successful Relationships at Home at Work and with Friends: Bringing Control Issues Under Control* (New York: Shaar Press, 2003), 13.
3. William Miller and Stephen Rollnick, *Motivational Interviewing: Preparing People for Change*, 2nd ed. (New York: Guilford Press, 2002).
4. Susan Jekielek and others, "Mentoring: A Promising Strategy for Youth Development," *Child Trends Research Brief*, February 2002, 3, http://mentoring.ca.gov/pdf/mentoringbrief2002.pdf.
5. Joseph P. Tierney and Jean Baldwin Grossman with Nancy Resch, *Making a Difference: An Impact Study of Big Brothers Big Sisters* (Philadelphia: Public/Private Ventures, 1995), 10.

CHAPTER 4

1. Dr. Chaim Ginott, *Between Parent and Child: The Bestselling Classic That Revolutionized Parent-Child Communication* (New York: Three Rivers Press, 1965), 8.

CHAPTER 5

1. Brenda Becker Oldstrom and others, "Caught in the Middle . . . Again," The Orchard Counseling, http://www.bloomington.in.us/~mark/caught.html.

2. Arlene F. Saluter and Terry A. Lugaila, "Marital Status and Living Arrangements: March 1996," Population Division, U.S. Bureau of the Census, no. P20 496, March 1998, http://www.census.gov/prod/3/98pubs/p20-496.pdf.

3. Patrick F. Fagan and Robert Rector, "The Effects of Divorce on America," The Heritage Center no. 1373 (June 5, 2000), http://www.nd.edu/~afreddos/papers/ fagan-divorce.htm.

Index

R

rebelliousness, 4, 26

reframing, 116–119

relationship-based parenting strategies, 1–2, 69–70

    drug and alcohol use/abuse, 131–132

    listening to nonsecular music, 127–128

    problems with prayer, 125

    rude behavior, 129–130

    school difficulties, 126

    smoking, 128–129

relationships. *See also* parents' relationship/marriage

    controlling, 58–59

    desire for deeper, 53

    investing in, 9–10

    reframing, 116–119

    teenagers' social, 15

relationship test, 38–39

Relationship Theory. *See also* relationship-based parenting strategies; Three Cs of Relationship Theory

    application of, 51–54

    breaking stalemates, 121

    for communication, 122–132

    improving communication, 91

    I = QR formula, 6

    for marital problems, 112–113

religion issues, 74–79

religious parents, challenges of raising children, 1–2

religious values, conflicting, 15–16

research

    depression in teens, 18–19

    development of adolescent brain, 14

    eating disorders in teens, 19

    mentoring relationships, 71–72

    positive/warm teen-parent relationships, 7–8

respect, 120–122

rude behavior, 129–130

S

salesperson versus CEO approach to parenting, 116–117

school difficulties, 125–126

school drop-outs, 109–113

secret dating, 48–54

secular music, 127–128

self-abusive behavior, 26

self-awareness, 63–64

self-esteem, 28, 29–30, 45–48

siblings of at-risk teens, 119

smoking, 128–129

stopping conversations, 92

students, ranking of problem issues, 8–9

About the Author

Rabbi Daniel Schonbuch holds a bachelor's degree from the Talmudic University of Florida and earned his rabbinic ordination at Yeshivat Knesset Beit Eliezer in Jerusalem. He then went on to become a Certified Alcohol and Substance Abuse Professional in New York State and is currently pursuing a masters degree in education.

Using his experience as former national education director of the National Council for Synagogue Youth, and his extensive work with teens at risk, Rabbi Schonbuch has turned his focus to "in-reach" and helping teens in the religious community struggling with issues of religion and identity. He is currently executive director of Shalom Task Force and maintains a private practice in family counseling in New York City.

Rabbi Schonbuch is a sought-after professional in the New York area. His writings appear on the Orthodox Union Web site and in numerous newspapers and magazines. He lives in New York City with his wife and children. You can reach Rabbi Schonbuch at www.neverbeyondreach.org or rabbischonbuch@yahoo.com.